CAN I
BE HONEST?

CAN I
BE HONEST?

*The Distorted Path of Sex,
Lies, and Healing*

SARAH TEMIMA

NAPLES, FL

Copyright © 2023 by Sarah Temima Becker
All rights reserved

Published in the United States by O'Leary Publishing
www.olearypublishing.com

The views, information, or opinions expressed in this book are solely those of the authors involved, and do not necessarily represent those of O'Leary Publishing, LLC.

The author has made every effort possible to ensure the accuracy of the information presented in this book. However, the information herein is sold without warranty, either expressed or implied. Neither the author, publisher, nor any dealer or distributor of this book will be held liable for any damages caused either directly or indirectly by the instructions or information contained in this book. You are encouraged to seek professional advice before taking any action mentioned herein.

All rights reserved. No part of this book may be reproduced or transmitted in any form by any means: electronic, mechanical, photocopy, recording, or other, without the prior and express written permission of the author, except for brief cited quotes. For information on getting permission for reprints and excerpts, contact: O'Leary Publishing.

ISBN: (print) 978-1-952491-57-3
ISBN: (ebook) 978-1-952491-58-0
Library of Congress Control Number: 2023910870

Developmental Editing by Heather Davis Desrocher
Line Editing by Kat Langenheim
Proofreading by Boris Boland
Cover and Interior Design by Jessica Angerstein
Printed in the United States of America

For my Ema

FOREWORD

My children are superheroes.

I mean, if you have children and you love them, I'm sure you think they're pretty great. And they are, because they're yours.

But mine are heroes. The fires they have walked through and how they've come out victorious can only be called miraculous.

Sarah Temima took a path of a specially curated hell. Some of which I knew, and much I did not. So is the reality of parenting.

The secrecy, the lies, the multiple lives – much in my child's story – well, it brought me to my knees.

She had the courage to share her life – heart wide open, fearless, and brave. The willingness to overcome herself again and again, to risk it all in the name of healing. That's my kind of superhero. That's my daughter.

And as I sit in the lush landscape of Hawaii, holding her belly growing with new life, I am in awe of who she chooses to be every day.

Because it is a choice, you know.

So can I be honest?

I was terrified of Sarah putting herself on the stake. Exposing herself, because that meant exposing me, my child, and what would that do to my life? To her life?

The truth is right here, in these pages.

It is messy, it is terrifying. It is raw, revealing the ugliness, the lies we tell ourselves, and the things we do to survive.

Some of it may be shocking; but if we are honest, I am sure you will find yourself somewhere in her story. When you were so lost in the depths of darkness – the light a distant memory – that you did what you thought you had to. Even with the keys in your own pocket, you couldn't find the way out.

So, I ask you to be kind, compassionate and loving as you absorb these pages. Hold the sacred space for her healing and your own. That's her purpose, her passion, her gift.

So Love On, my beautiful girl.

I am now, and forever will be, your greatest champion. I will stand and hold you with the fiercest love in the center of the fire, again and again.

We are the Phoenix rising, by choice.

Always, all ways, loving you.

Ema

(PS – Hold on to your tits.)

INTRODUCTION

6\10\22 Canggu, Bali, Indonesia

The terrifying talent of a pathological liar is to be so absolutely sure that our lies are the truth, that we forget what the truth actually is.

And so after many years of living lies that I had masterfully convinced myself were the truth, the scariest part of writing this book was knowing I would have to tell the *real* truth, the whole way through.

Part of harvesting my story was to hear it for myself and get it out of my body. It felt like the final wringing of a damp and dirty sponge.

Fabrication is just as much a talent as it is the shadow side of an artist. We can create any story and make it true – dressing it up so seductively that it pulls you in. *Intrinsic* truth, as we come home to it without fluff and decor, leaves us naked and humiliated before offering its aid and guiding us to grace.

I have contemplated sharing what really happened. *How would my truth be received? What if all the people who claimed to be inspired by my authenticity learned what my journey really looked like? What if they were actually **repelled and shocked?***

These fears were about more than ruining people's perceptions of me. I was also afraid, because – although I have finally come to embrace and live in my truth – I knew that writing this book and revisiting my past would lead me to unveil parts of myself that were possibly still in the dark.

Naturally, the writing process poses a challenge, evoking pain and old wounds. I relived trauma for the sake of healing it, in hopes that the words would reach the right hands. The buried past started making its way to the surface quickly. Unnamed faces and places, stomach-turning events, and people I no longer associate with begged to be excavated and acknowledged.

I had to slowly uncover my eyes, finger by finger, and look intently at all the things I had chosen to actively conceal and ignore. There were truths uncovered just recently, as I asked new questions while looking for all the information necessary for each page.

In times past, the anxiety – brought on by memories filled with shame – was so overpowering and had such a grip on me that I began to question whether I would survive.

Every once in a while, when I was seemingly buried in the lies, taking my life felt like the only real solution. I could see no other way. Knowing the things I have done, I could not love myself, and could not imagine being loved by someone else.

I could not see or **feel** the truth, and it made my sanity more and more unsteady. Every last one of my relationships was strained in some way – as a daughter, a sister, a friend, a lover, or as anything at all. My entire life was like a job that I dreaded going to every day.

Worst of all, I was pretty sure everyone knew it. It was as if I kept up the act for no one but myself. Everyone had some sort of wary feeling towards me – a feeling that they could not fully trust me, even if they didn't know why.

Once, at a workshop I attended in New York City, there was a mandatory exercise where the participants had to walk around the room, and then stop and look into a random person's eyes for three seconds. Then they were to say one of three things: "I trust you," or "I don't trust you," or "I'm not sure if I trust you."

When they came to me, every single person in the room said, "I don't trust you." Thirteen times, from thirteen strangers, I heard this – in the space of just a few minutes.

For some reason, it stung way more than when someone I knew personally said it. These were strangers; they did not know me, yet they were all certain that I could not be trusted. It was a stench that I couldn't wash off. Soap could not touch it. Not even with a loofah and lather.

After everything, though, I have arrived – and I have absolutely no regrets or fantasies about a re-do. I am so in love with the divine orchestration of my life; if any piece had been different, I would not be standing here as is. And I love who I have become.

Today I am a fiercely devoted woman – to truth, to love, to kindness, to full expression – and most importantly, living freely and authentically in my body.

I understand that some believe in total privacy, not sharing intimate details of their lives. However, *I* unquestionably believe that I lived this chapter of my life – and miraculously exited the chaos alive and well – to offer it as a message.

I have now centered my existence around loving myself so intimately, that every single version of me, every choice, and every ounce of humiliation that my sacred temple has endured, is loved.

All of me is loved.

My prayer is that you read my story with your heart wide open. If I can love on the shamed parts of myself today and breathe deeply with them, maybe you can love on those parts of you, too.

Note: Every single detail in this book is 100 percent true.

And though you might wonder if it is exaggerated, please know that I made every effort *not* to exaggerate – even in the slightest – due to my personal agreement with the truth.

My commitment to you while sharing this story is to give you the raw-boned and unfiltered reality. Sometimes my reality was simply as theatrical as it sounds.

As I take this pilgrimage of recounting my past, I will walk a parallel journey with you. Insights, reflections, questions, and lessons learned will follow along delicately, shining a brighter light on experiences that once seemed unavailing.

A vengeful part of me did not want to hide the real names of the people mentioned in this book. However, when I noticed that my ego was wanting to prove something, and felt the excitement that rose in my stomach when I thought of how much more attention the book could get, I decided against it.

I said a big "fuck you" to that little voice, and I reminded myself that my ego is not what the story is about.

So, yes, most names (and lines of work) have been changed. Not necessarily to protect anyone's privacy, but simply to keep our attention on the message, not the gossip.

As much as I ache to tell it all, it is impossible to fit all the details of my life into this one book. So, if questions arise – even if you are a stranger or someone from my past who would like clarity – please do not hesitate to write to me. I would love to clear any confusion or hurt, and I promise you the whole truth.

Now let's start from the beginning.

A woman's entire life is a ceremony.

- Unknown

I was born in the hills of Jerusalem in 1993. "Woah, no way!" is usually the reaction when I tell someone this. There is a fascination that Americans have with foreigners.

Of course, there were many events that took place leading up to my birth. It goes for all of us without saying: it's a miracle that we are here at all.

My parents both migrated to Israel from the United States in their late teens – my father from West Virginia, and my mother from Valley Stream,

Long Island. They met soon afterward at a mutual friend's house party. My dad remembers it all vividly. My mother walked in late, kindle-eyed with an equally beaming smile. Everyone at the party was circled up in the living room, smoking and enjoying the usual party banter, along with music and the passing of joints.

Without missing a beat, my mother began walking around the circle, greeting and hugging every single person until she reached my father, who was strumming away with a sound like a young James Taylor. She took her time with each hug that she gave, exuding loving kindness. My father watched her grace, intensely. As she leaned in and landed her last hug on him, he was smitten.

Many years later, I learned that my father was married to another woman at that time. He and the unnamed woman were in a separation period, living apart. They had only been married for about a year. When my parents started seeing each other, my father filed divorce papers.

My parents married six months after they met.

Fortunately, two weeks before their wedding, the divorce papers from his previous marriage came back signed and sealed.

The technicality of the adultery draws me in, as I reminisce on when and why I became a dishonest lover, many years down the road.

Something in me allowed for it.

I do not hold my parents liable in any way, nor am I excusing myself from my personal choices. Still, it is illuminating to see the dishonesty as one of the cycles that my family repeated for generations. We repeat them until someone points at it and dissolves the seemingly endless loop.

When hearing the news of the engagement, my grandparents, as a wedding gift, flew my parents back to the States. There was a small ceremony at a local synagogue; family and friends surrounded the newlyweds as the rabbi dubbed them Man and Wife.

The first place my parents lived after the wedding was a run-down apartment in Jerusalem on King George Road. Their first child, my older sister Esther, was born soon after.

It was during the Gulf War, and my dad was busking on the street to keep the family fed. Since his early teens, he had stood firm in his beliefs regarding freedom from "the system." Obligatory bills, nine-to-fives, or any legitimate jobs were not in his interest. It created an incredible challenge for my parents; but they were young and in love, and devoted to their sovereignty.

Somehow they made it through – always due to a miracle or a random act of charity that saved them when they needed help the most.

My mother shared a memory with me recently about when she was pregnant with Esther. She was craving chocolate, and they only had 10 shekel left (a little less than $3 US.) She and my dad took a walk to the store, and when they went to pay, the total was nine shekel. They bought the chocolate anyway, trusting that they would be divinely guided to their next meal.

I look at that story now and consider what other tendencies or patterns are passed down to our children. My mother fell, full tilt, for a poverty-stricken musician. Later on, I too fell for a man just like that

– a few times. And my brother **became** a poverty-stricken musician for many years, before climbing his way out of the deep, mirrored well that was his father's reflection.

It's interesting to look at our past from a new angle, gaining a deeper understanding of the themes that run in our bloodline and the stories that are passed down.

However, genetics and poverty, or genetics and addiction, do not necessarily go hand in hand. According to studies, and an interview with physician and addiction expert Dr. Gabor Mate, there is no gene that determines that you will be an alcoholic if your father and grandfather were alcoholics. It is merely the trauma repeatedly experienced by the children of these people that creates addictions and dangerous behaviors. There are brothers born to the same alcoholic father; one goes down the path of alcoholism, but the other one stays healthy and happy on the other side of town. It is our environment and the choices that we make that lead us to our destiny. Our parents and their ways do not have a grip on us in the way we might be accustomed to thinking.

On the brighter side, because of what I learned from parents who lived in such a state of trust, I became a woman who manifests **everything.** It was passed down that we were always supported. The universe had our backs.

During the war, it was a frequent occasion for my mother and father to have to run to the designated sealed room when the alarms went off. If they blared, it meant missiles were targeting Israel, and they needed to move quickly. It was a one-bedroom apartment, so the bedroom was chosen as the safe haven. The windows and door were sealed with duct tape. My mother was eight months pregnant, wearing a gas mask.

They lived that way for some time. One day, when Esther was a little baby, she was napping in her stroller on the balcony. When my mother took her inside, she smelled the familiar stench of gasoline fumes covering her daughter's skin. She knew it was time to leave the city. But the decision was technically made for them when they found an eviction notice on their door. It was not a surprise, with multiple months having passed with the rent not paid.

At that point, it had been a couple years since my mom had seen her parents, so my grandparents covered the expenses for her to come with Esther for a visit. "When I get back, please have a home for us," my mother requested before kissing my father goodbye.

When she returned a few weeks later from the trip, my father indeed surprised her with their new home – a cave in a small town called Beit Meir. Yes, it was an actual cave, in the hills – I am not making an exaggerated reference to a small studio apartment in New York City. This particular cave had stone walls, zero plumbing (no toilet at all) and no electricity. My father thought it was absolutely perfect – another win against the system.

He had a donkey named Blue, and my father had the animal carry a mattress, a portable crib, and a wooden stove up to the cave. My parents siphoned water from the hills, and they ate eggs from friends' farms that were cracked and not saleable.

My dad with Blue, early 90's

I am fascinated by these pieces of history, and commend my parents for their dedication and faith in divine guidance. I share as much as I know about that period in time, based on what my parents have been gracious enough to share with me. Still, their kind of conviction is something many of us have only heard of in folk tales and Bible stories. They took it pretty far – some might say that they put their own well-being, along with their children's, at risk.

Did they see it that way? To them, the system was more dangerous than hunger and poverty. I think they were just trying to claim that basic human right of independence and freedom.

For a long time, I thought it was my parents' mutual desire to live this way; but my mother recently admitted that she was just so young, proud, and broke. The deeper truth was that my father's voice and beliefs were too loud for her to hear her own.

I have learned a lot about the consciousness we have before we are physically birthed into this world. Some say babies can feel and understand everything, from conception to the canal. Sunni

Karll, author of *Sacred Birthing*, dives deep into the conversation of babies and their ability to feel more than we have been taught to believe.

I was conceived in the cave following the war, with poverty all around. Did that affect me as an adult? Did I experience trauma from it? These are questions I ask without receiving a specific answer, and maybe I will never truly know. I do believe it is possible that unborn and newborn babies are listening to every thought and every word spoken, and above all, I believe they feel the energy in the labor room.

Many adults claim to remember their birth after undergoing hypnosis, or during a simple meditation where the memory is evoked. Grown men and women have recounted the first events that led them into lives filled with fear, sadness, learning disabilities, and more. As adults, they accurately remember things like induction, epidurals, the forceps, and even a doctor who came to work drunk. It is worth it to inquire, as most of us now live in a privileged time that allows for more questioning regarding old ways and programs. We are **all** waking up and getting curious.

My parents lived peacefully in that cave for months – until, soon after my conception there, a revolutionary movement with extreme Zionists began to stir.

> **Zionism, political ideology**
> Zionism is a nationalist movement that espouses the establishment of, and support for, a homeland for the Jewish people centered in the area roughly corresponding to the Land of Israel, the region of Palestine, Canaan, or the Holy Land, on the basis of a long Jewish connection and attachment to that land.

At the time, a major newspaper article was published, featuring Zionists living in caves and awaiting the Messiah. My parents were pictured on the front page, but they did not intend to be involved in the movement. They were just broke and wanted to be left alone. Somehow, they found themselves being instruments in a much larger political scheme than they would have liked.

My mother in the cave, Beit Meir, 1993

An article with my father and mother holding my older sister, Esther, in the cave, Beit Meir, 1993

This article alerted Beit Meir to my parents' living situation. On the same day that other journalists arrived for some comments and photographs, a few men from the nearby town came to have a talk with my father. They were trying to get him to leave the area while a journalist was trying to interview him. The presence of the journalists turned out to be a good thing, because those town men had planned on taking my father by force.

These men, along with the townspeople they represented, were angry at my parents for living for free – avoiding taxes and the Jewish communal duties. The townspeople's irritation, along with the publicity from the article, left my parents no choice but to leave the cave.

A local family heard about the now homeless young couple with a 2-year-old daughter and a baby on the way. Taking pity on us, they let my family stay in one of their empty houses for a while. It was lucky that they did, because on December 29, 1993, I was on the way.

22 CAN I BE HONEST?

*The verbal altercation, my father below,
the townsmen above, 1993*

My mother found a ride to a friend's cottage in the hills for my delivery. She held my father's hand and practiced her breathing while she waited for the midwife.

This friend owned a harp business, and she decided to play the harp quietly near my mother while she pushed.

"Turn that fucking thing OFF!" my mother screamed.

I guess that even the sweetest sounds might drive a woman crazy when she is in labor.

One day, when I was 6 months old with raging chickenpox that had spread to my mother, my dad had a chat with his friends in town. The conversation was about a company that was in the midst of a building project, and the company was looking for young Jewish families to fill the new houses. But the government was threatening to destroy the houses, and so the company needed people in them as quickly as possible.

I guess my parents did not ask too many questions. They needed somewhere to live – pronto. They had learned they were overstaying their welcome at the local family's home.

The only things that my parents had heard about the new development was that it was a young, hip and religious community. When my dad went home to talk it all over with my mom, she followed his lead.

Shortly after, they moved into a two-bedroom house in a small biblical city called Shiloh, with a backyard view of Palestinian residences.

Recently, I learned a lot about what was going on during this time. I discerned the events more acutely when I removed the loaded stories, and outlined some of the facts. I understand now that I only had Israel's version – what we heard in school, the tales shared in circles during holiday gatherings, and what the Torah outlined for us.

> To·rah
> /ˈtōrə/ noun
> (in Judaism) the law of God as revealed to Moses and recorded in the first five books of the Hebrew scriptures

I was told by my elders that it was **our** land; that God said so.

Stepping into adulthood today, I cannot grasp the concept of **war** started over **land.** I cannot fathom **bloodshed, terror, and ownership** over **earth,** as if it is anyone's to possess. I cannot make sense of **taking** someone's home by force.

I am actively unlearning and reprogramming what religion has placed in my psyche.

I have always stayed as far away from politics and religion as possible, once I was old enough to walk away. However, I still understand that I am an Israeli-born woman, and Jewish by blood.

I say this with conviction – I am **completely removed.** I place no label on myself, nor do I belong to any group of people. I am queer, which by definition is anything "other than the norm" or "unusual" or "eccentric" or "unconventional."

I am devastated at the lives lost **on both sides.** Shivers travel down my spine at the thought of anyone murdering innocent people in the name of God, or for land.

Is there not room for everyone?

I deeply, deeply mourn the people of Israel whose lives were lost to terrorism, suicide bombers, and violent extremists.

Fortunately, I myself have missed a train that was later blown up by a suicide bomber. I have awakened from a nap on a bus to a rock being thrown at my window. I have seen horrific things with my own eyes. And my sisters have witnessed shootings and stabbings in their periphery.

I also know that it takes two.

I do not stand for anything but peace.

I want nothing more than harmony, unity and forgiveness. I don't know how all of that can be possible after all the trauma, but I can still pray, can't I?

In any case, at the time of my parents' move to the West Bank in the early 1990's, Israel was negotiating with the United States. The US was going to loan Israel $10 billion if Israel agreed to a freeze on the construction of all settlements in the West Bank and the Gaza Strip. Israel was resistant, and ended up doing only a **partial** freeze on construction. Still, the US president authorized the loan guarantee, without Israel committing to a **total** freeze on settlements. The negotiations were between 1993 and 1995, and evidently they were the reason behind the construction of homes and also the quick threat of demolition. The country was in the middle of contract negotiations – and things were messy.

The rent my parents paid was paid to the Yishuv (or "settlement in the Land of Israel," and also the name for the city's council). The council did not legally own the homes.

The rent was not even really rent; the amount was about $40 US a month. The English-speaking community there made life easier.

My brother, Levi Chai Avraham, was born 22 months after my arrival. And then last, but not least – a sister, Hadar Miriam Shacharit, arrived right at the tail end of our life in Israel. There were four of us – all thick as thieves.

My mom gave massages (she was certified since the age of 18), sold eggs, cleaned houses, and watched the neighbors' kids to help earn money. My dad would stay over in Jerusalem and play music gigs, or get a construction job here and there.

His dreams of being a musician took over much of his time – and at home, he was often invisible, like the character mentioned in a song from the Broadway show Chicago, Mr. Cellophane. He may have been on the couch, but we did not always know it.

Shiloh, 1998. (left) Esther, my father, Levi, and me

As an adult, I can see that my need for male validation and attention could have easily stemmed from the way my father was not emotionally available. When he was in the room, we would try to get his attention – but we soon learned to just leave him alone. His aloofness – mixed with vodka – created a disinterest and disconnect, which was felt by all.

While writing this book, I took great care to not paint my dad as the bad guy. Today, we have an increasingly connected relationship, as I dissipate the anger that was geared towards him. As we put all the pieces together through phone calls and voice notes, things become more crystallized, and I remove the judgment in my tone. My heart has softened, and I forgive myself for any negative portrayals that I composed. I also have forgiven him for any pain that his choices caused my family.

However, the truth will always win, and what I share is simply that. My father today acknowledges his neglect that eventually led to the separation of our family.

In the background of my family dynamics, there was still a political game playing out. When the

Yishuv started pressing for higher rent, my father defiantly stopped paying altogether. Even the electricity was stolen by the Yishuv, and the payments were pocketed.

My father is a highly intelligent man. Knowing his rights and the legal system, he was aware that it would be a lot worse for the Yishuv than for him if the government found out that they were charging families rent on homes they did not actually own.

My father carried on and continued working with his musician buddies, losing himself in ambitious plans to put music projects together.

He started ripping up all bills that came in the mail, certain that he was not required to pay. His rage against the system grew daily, and we had less and less money on which to live.

When the Purim holiday rolled around (kind of like a Jewish Halloween, where costumes are a tradition), my mother, using scissors, would cut up a cardboard box into the shape of wings. With a layer of glue, she would add sparkles and other inventive decorations. She would then staple hair ties into the center of the wings and add more color. Voila. I was a butterfly. She really knew how to make it all work with so little.

We had one store in our town, the Makolet. Everything else required a two-hour bus ride or an hour in a car. We usually did not have money for the bus and did not own a car, so our necessities came from that little corner store most of the time – things like eggs, milk, bread, and treats.

Every Friday, we would get a 'Shabbat treat' from the store before candles were lit to bring in the holy day – a piece of chocolate or small candy. It was the best moment of the whole week, and we always looked forward to it.

Once, when I was about 4, I found a shekel on the ground right in front of that little store. I remember my eyes combusting with delight. I kissed the shekel discreetly, then held it to my chest as if protecting its life.

I walked around the store carefully eyeing the shelves up and down. I felt rich and thought, I can get anything I want. I left with a long, snake-shaped gummy candy, and I was the happiest little girl in the world.

My home-spun butterfly costume, Shiloh

I was always a sensitive child. Tears filled my eyes easily – even in preschool. Just witnessing a classmate's emotions was a tender moment for me.

Around the same time that I found that shekel, a boy sat across from me in a class where we were learning about blending colors with paint.

White and dark purple created lavender, white and red created pink. I loved that class.

The boy was sitting in his chair, looking around with eyes welled up and a quivering frown. I can still see his exact face and features as if I was staring at him in real time, over 20 years later. His eyes seemed so lost and broken. He had soft, caramel features, and his feet dangled in the air a few inches above the ground while he sat. He was so young; today, I imagine he had a hard life at home. Maybe his father was aggressive rather than neglectful like mine, or maybe his mother was absent. Sadness moved through me, entering my body as if it was my own.

Taking it all in, interpreting it in whatever way that my 4-year-old mind was capable, I felt my own tears arise. I walked over to him and offered him some of my cucumber snacks. I needed him to smile.

For the first time in my life, I detected the incandescent burn in my chest that I would feel countless times following this notable moment. That sting was empathy.

Later on, I would lose it for a long time when my body froze over – checking into survival mode, disconnecting me, locking me into a place where the only pain, sadness or despair I could feel was my own. I came to believe that inherent empathy was irredeemable.

When I was 5, I had my first sleepover with one of my best friends; I'll call her Z. We were next door neighbors, and our mothers were good friends. Z was a year younger than me. A little before dawn, I woke up from my sleep to the sound of her climbing out of my bedroom window.

Purim in Israel

I rubbed my eyes, making sure that it was really happening. Slowly, my confusion turned to hurt and worry. Did I do something?

"Wuttsa matter?" I asked her, leaning out of the window.

"I wanna go home to my mommy."

I stayed silent while I held my composure and watched her scurry over to her house. I got back into bed, feeling the familiar burn and shedding tears. *It must be me*, I thought.

Aside from me being extremely sensitive, there was an early curiosity of sexuality brewing. What is unclear is where it originated. I have no memories of any adults being inappropriate. I never saw anything on TV that might have generated the interest; we never had television.

The first time I played "doctor," I was in kindergarten. (Where could I have learned this game? And why did I want someone to look at my vagina – or want to examine theirs?)

I remember laying down on a flat bed of some sort that was in the park where a classmate and I were playing during recess. When I squinted hard enough, it seemed the teacher was out of sight. I was clearly still too young to understand depth perception.

I do not know what exactly we were looking for underneath our underwear, but we were certain it was something interesting. I'm not sure if the teacher ever told my mother, but we most definitely got caught – and were pulled apart. Then we were given a good old-fashioned time out.

The second time was in Z's house, and the events unfolded identically – except this time, I moved fast enough to pretend like we were playing a more appropriate game when her mom walked in.

My sneaky behavior was cooking early. I later realized that innocent curiosity leads to deception when we feel we cannot explore something because an authority labels it bad, or punishes us for it. That fact is apparent in this story, because I learned to hide what we were doing.

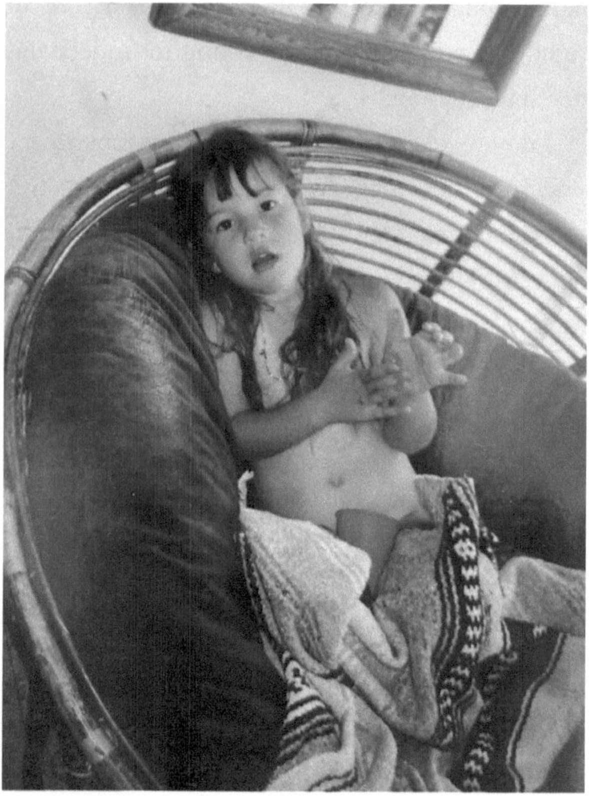

Shiloh, 1998

Meanwhile, my parents' relationship was slowly unraveling. Poverty, along with my father's neglect and substance abuse, were the main ingredients in the soup of discord.

The memories I have of my father from the years in Israel are mostly correlated to music. I recall the sound of a slide on an acoustic guitar, along with an electric guitar and harmonica. I have hazy images of him sitting near his instruments, smoking cigarettes, his hands stained with white paint from his construction jobs.

When my grandparents came to visit, they had big plans for a typical vacation with their daughter and their grandkids – road trips, ice cream, beach days. What they did not know was that my mother just needed food.

When they realized the severity of the situation, they took her aside and worriedly asked, "Honey, do you need to come back to America with us? We'll take care of you."

But she was too proud. "This is my home, and this is my husband." She could not bear to admit how bad it really was.

She actually did try to leave a couple of times. One time, determined and ready, she packed up and left while he was out at a gig in the city.

After battling her decision of taking the kids from their father, and experiencing the fear of being out on the street, she caved and returned. However, the night had already passed, and it was early morning when she dragged herself back.

She looked around, defeated. She realized he had never even come home, so he never knew she left.

Since I was 16, my mother has been telling me that I am her twin, walking faithfully in her footsteps. It was as if the route had been laid out for me and all I had to do was follow the tracks in the mud.

The pattern of leaving and coming back brings me to the later memory of all the wobbly relationships in which I found myself down the line. "On and off" was my MO – break up, then get back together. When I would leave someone, I always felt so sure, empowered, and liberated. Then, somehow I would get sucked back in, after receiving an apologetic phone call – or simply by raising my own white flag, choosing toxicity over being alone.

Shortly after my mother tried to leave my father, a call came. My grandmother, my father's mother, was dying. My parents were hanging on by a thread, and my father was staying mostly in a caravan across the street that his friend had loaned him. There, he would play his music, drink, and sidestep.

Since my father was out, my mom took the call. My grandfather said to her, "It's not looking good, he needs to come see her as soon as possible."

My dad was in the city looking for work that day, and my mother hurried to find him a ticket back to the States so that all arrangements would be ready when he returned. She called friends and asked to borrow money, and booked the ticket right away for him. When he got home that evening and she told him the news, instead of thanking her, he went into a paranoid rage. He accused her of buying the ticket just to get rid of him.

She knew she needed to leave.

By the time I was 6 years old, my father's habits and his precarious lifestyle had become too much for my mother. She was extremely unhappy, and she was worried for our well-being.

My parents hid it well, because my memory is clear of fights or anything out of control. Evidently, my father's style was checked-out and distant, rather than belligerent.

I still loved him deeply.

It was the year 2000, and things were getting bad in the Palestinian territory that we were occupying. Aside from the marital combustion at home, buses were being blown up, the hills were on fire, and shootings occurred in the middle of the road.

My maternal grandparents insisted that my family come to the US and take some time off from the horrid events in the Middle East.

Quickly, we were all packed up and ready to go. At the last minute, my father said, "You know what? I don't want to be on your parents' tab.

I'm going to stay back. Someone needs to watch the house."

It is comical how every story has two sides, especially the pivotal ones that define a moment. My mother says he changed his mind last-minute; yet my father says he was never invited. I will leave it up to you to feel the truth.

He packed us in the car and waved goodbye. We had round-trip tickets, so there was no fuss. We would be back in a couple of months. My mother had $50 in her pocket, four kids, and one suitcase.

It is 2022 as I am writing this. We never went back, and my dad has been living in that same house as a squatter for nearly 30 years.

> squat·ter
> /skwädər/
> A person who unlawfully occupies an uninhabited building or unused land.

When we first arrived on US soil, we spent some time at my grandparents' house in New Jersey so that my mom could get on her feet. They lived in a calm, pleasant senior home community. They had weekly bingo, and shuffleboard near the pool, and I loved playing that game while getting my cheeks pinched by the elders.

When the six-month point rolled around and my mother had not returned to Israel, my father started asking questions. He had been okay with her leaving for a little while at first, knowing that the war took a toll on everyone. It had made sense for us to get some space away from it. He was not yet aware of how his behavior had led her to remain in the States.

We were still very young. I was only 6 years old. My brother, Levi, was 4. My little sister, Hadar, was still an infant, and my older sister, Esther, was 9. Esther was the only one old enough to really understand what was happening, and she carried a lot of that weight in the family for years. She was "Mommy number two" in many ways.

My relationship with Esther was never warm while we were children. Starting when she was about 10, we cultivated a "battle of the big sisters" dynamic. Physical fights were frequent between us. I have a memory of her throwing an alarm clock at my face in the morning, and another of her pulling my hair. And I was always filled with terror whenever she would chase me. I now take full responsibility for the fact that I tested her. I would come up behind her, push her if she triggered me, and then run for my life – knowing her retaliation would be fierce. She was always smaller than I was, but she was stronger, older, and colder.

Doors were slammed in my face, and there was always aggression and cattiness. Hadar and Levi were constantly pulling us off of each other.

I promised myself that I would make sure my relationship with my little sister would look nothing like what I had with Esther. I mostly held to that promise, building a loving relationship with Hadar and doing my best to be a good role model. I totally fumbled the role-model ball when she started going to clubs at 14, lying religiously, and seeking male validation. I was devastated, facing the hard truth that it was more than partly my fault.

We went about our days with a question. "Where's *Abba*? Is he gonna come visit?" we would occasionally ask.

Maybe we would get a kiss and a hug and a nonchalant answer. But we always went back to playing or whatever we were doing, feeling certain we would see him soon and that everything was OK.

I was starstruck by America. It seemed a lot cooler than Israel right off the boat. My *bubby* had all the bright-colored and mouthwatering cereals that we had never seen before: Frosted Flakes, Cap'n Crunch, **and** Cinnamon Toast Crunch. It was so different for us to be getting those expensive, so-called high-quality cereals. They had so much flavor than what we were used to! We even got to have Coca-Cola and Chinese food, like real Americans.

Being introduced to processed foods – to excess – when we had mostly been eating small amounts of organic or local foods was a major change. My mother was always health-conscious, even when there was little that she could afford.

Today, I feel a newfound gratitude about the seeds my mother planted. But back then, we were just kids, ignorant of mind and envious of others who got to have junk food.

Now I see what she did for us. Though I was on and off in maintaining a healthy lifestyle after my childhood, I always had a grounding in eating healthy foods. It was a truth and an inner knowing that would bring me back every time I fell off the path. It was a profound reminder, a guiding light in the darkest days. All the damage that I did to my body with drugs, alcohol, and chemicals was healed with the support of organic and whole foods – a return to nature.

"Ema, puh-leeeeeez!" We would whine and beg my mother for the junk food until she gave in; but usually, bubby would just make the call for her, always saying **yes.**

My grandmother was an amazing woman. She was the type of grandmother that made you feel warm, loved, and spoiled. She was kind, funny, and affectionate in all the right ways. I loved burying my head into her chest when she held me.

"I just want to make it to 50 years with your mommy," my grandfather would say to his daughter – my mother. They did make it to 50, right before he passed.

Though secrets were kept in that family too, the love between my grandparents trumped all.

It was heartbreaking to learn, many years after her death, that my grandmother suffered from a great deal of severe trauma. I have battled with myself over whether that information would be important to include in this book, considering that I am dissecting the generational trauma in my lineage. I came to the conclusion that the details of that particular story are not mine to tell. I believe that if my ancestors wanted their stories to be told, I would know it. Telling my grandmother's story would involve endless research, and big conversations. My grandmother had complex and controversial parents, two siblings, four children, a handful of cousins, and over 20 grandchildren. I humbly bowed out of that task.

My grandfather was a good man. However, he was a little tougher than my grandmother. I was afraid of him and his rules. If I sipped soda right from the can, he would snatch it away. Then – with a stern look that made me turn to my mother for consolation – he would show me how to pour it into a glass.

I would like to take a moment to honor my grandfather. He served in World War II, and during his service, he got word that his brother, Louis, was missing in action. My heroic grandfather went out many times to search and find out if Louis was alive. He even reenlisted after he finished out his military contract for the sole purpose of continuing his search.

On the last time out, when his unit decided they could no longer be able to give him a jeep or supplies to search, he finally found Louis' name on a prisoner of war list in a small village in Italy. They exhumed Louis' body, and the whole village escorted them and threw flowers onto the cart. Not only did my grandfather come home with Louis for a proper burial, but he also continued searching and found the bodies of countless other unclaimed soldiers. He helped return them to their mourning families back in America. I am grateful and humbled to be this valiant man's granddaughter.

While we were staying at my grandparents' place, my mother slept on the couch, and my three siblings and I shared two beds in the guest room. Still, the decor and updated appliances gave me the impression of real luxury – and to my young eyes, it absolutely was.

Everything seemed extremely shiny and cozy there. The carpeted living room floor was a particular slice of heaven for me – especially when we got to watch cartoons on TV there for the first time. I would sprawl out for hours, making imaginary angel wings into the fluff.

When we spent time at the seniors' community pool, I remember feeling in awe of the 17-year-old lifeguard in her red, one-piece bathing suit. She fascinated me. It was like she had walked straight out of a movie. I was just shy of 7 years old, but I was fixated on becoming something just like that when I was older.

Once it was settled that we were staying in America for longer than was originally planned, my mom knew she needed to get on her own two feet. She had some connections in a small suburban town in New York called Monsey.

After leaving my grandparents' house, our first home in Monsey was in the basement of an odd young couple's house. For some reason, I remember the wife as a crabby old cat lady. Funny enough, we actually found a dead cat in the closet on our move-in day.

It was the five of us in a one-bedroom apartment. Although we were always a close family group, sometimes it was **too** close, and we did not always like that very much.

My memory travels back to the bedroom of that apartment. I remember that my mother read bedtime stories under the "forts" that we created with the sheets. We were high-energy kids, with a lot of laughter and play. Love was definitely always present.

Like any parent, my mother carried guilt about all the years raising her children – when she was emotionally lost and stuck in scarcity. Once I was old enough to understand, she would drop her head with shame while sharing her inner world with me. She wondered if she had "messed us up" with all the choices that she and my father had made. I always shook my head, wishing that she understood what a gift and opportunity we received – we were able to rise from the ashes.

Did we have an incredibly challenging time? Absolutely. Did we become wildly passionate and strong individuals with unique personalities and gifts? 1000 percent yes. No "normal" upbringing would have created the diamonds that my siblings and I are today.

I honor my mother for doing whatever was necessary to keep us breathing and fed. She did more than that, too – she introduced us to spirituality, showered us with affection, taught us about independence, educated us about healthy ways of eating, and fostered true human-to-human connection among us from the time we were in diapers.

To this day, my siblings are my best friends.

Still, we had to move through incredibly challenging times of rugged living, drought, and depressions before seeing a way out.

In Judaism, as in any religion, marriage is sacred. Though my mother knew in her heart that she was done with her marriage, the new Jewish community in Monsey did what they could to help salvage it. The rabbi from the local synagogue, along with some communal help, raised money to buy my father a ticket to come and see us.

The local Jewish community was determined to get my parents into some marriage counseling and save the relationship. But when my father arrived, my mother still did not allow him to stay with us.

Any questions he had about "why" were not answered. She was already spent.

The local community found a place for him to stay – a room in someone's house. He still had to pay a nightly fee, so they even got him some construction work to pass the time while we were in school. He would walk to the jobs, miles at a time, trucking paint buckets and brushes back and forth.

"I don't know what I was doing, I just knew I wanted to save the marriage. I did what I was told," he says.

After about a month of a Jewish version of marriage counseling (meeting the rabbi in a back room of the synagogue) and spending some quality time with us (watching cartoons for hours, when my mother allowed it), my father decided he needed to head back to Israel.

"I need to guard the house," he explained. "Let me know when you make a decision," he said to my mother.

And just like that, he left.

The next time he came to visit was a little while later, after my mother called him and said that she was ready for a divorce. In Judaism, there is something called a **get,** which is a Jewish version of a divorce. Under Jewish law, a woman can only divorce her husband with his permission.

My father is far from evil, and the last thing he wanted was to deny a woman her true rights. Nevertheless, the rules say that the **get** must be presented in a room of witnesses, with both parties present. Again, my father got on a plane, but this time it was just for the purpose of getting the **get** and then flying back to Israel.

They both agreed that they had something to say to their kids.

They sat us down in a circle, and said, "Do you guys know what a divorce is? It means we are not going to be living together anymore. And since *Abba* is going back to Israel, we won't be seeing him unless he can come visit." My mother added, "He still loves you so much."

The look on Esther's face was of devastation. She knew exactly what it meant. The rest of us were still too young to fully comprehend.

The next day, my dad got on a plane – and when he got home after his 13-hour flight, he screamed and howled on the floor for three days straight. Something happened to him that day – the sober realization sunk in that we were really gone.

From that time on, sobriety was not a state of mind in which my father had any interest.

Rage took over, and he felt he had nothing to live for. He made a decision to take out the anger on his body, the government, and the Yishuv. He was going to make sure the house could not be taken from him. It was all he had left.

He went to the mayor and made a case about how the Yishuv endangered the lives of the residents, putting the people in the front lines of a war zone. The mayor heard my father, and signed a paper renouncing any rights to ask him for money. The mayor also handed my father a few thousand shekels, paying him back for the seven years that he had paid rent to the Yishuv. The Mayor agreed that absolutely nothing was legal about the situation.

As I sit here and write out these details of my parents' history and ways of living, I ponder why all of this is relevant to my story. *Isn't this their shit? Shouldn't I stay on my personal experiences in my memoir?* My response to that little voice is: I believe that the witnessing of those family events – whether from hearing, seeing, or even just being their kin – eventually led to a lot of programming. My brain was receiving and taking negative notes of what I witnessed and found to be true regarding society, authority, men, money, and success. A mindset of scarcity, along with a belief that life does not turn out the way it is planned, created certain perceptions that crept into my own neuro-pathways. They attached themselves to my psyche, and eventually shaped who I became, what my beliefs were, and choices that I made.

I never correlated the events of leaving my dad and moving to the States with the word "trauma." Many years later, in my teens, a therapist asked me, "How did the trauma of being taken at a young age to a new country impact you?"

I looked at her like she was crazy. "That's not trauma, lady," I replied. "Trauma is watching your family get slaughtered in front of you, or getting viciously raped." That really was what I thought about it, and I was slightly offended that she put me in the category of having been **traumatized.**

I have an unsettled relationship with the word now. The dictionary's definition of **trauma** is "a deeply distressing or disturbing experience." I think we are all deeply traumatized in some way if that is the definition we are using. Our whole species is distressed and disturbed.

For a long time, I blamed my father for what had happened, and I stacked every detail that I could think of onto a sky-high pile about why he was the typical absent, alcoholic father. I loved holding onto those reasons; they were my excuse.

The specific events that took place around why and how we left Israel is a raw topic – and always has been. I did not hear both of my parents' sides of the story until recently, when I called them for information to include in this book.

We had a house full of secrets, and nobody knew exactly what had happened. We went along with the particular narratives shown to us. We took note of events as they were explained and processed through our youthful minds. We were given petite pieces of information, with sugar coating glazed onto every syllable.

I know that my parents did not intend to keep so much from us. We were just so young. How could they share all of it with our innocent hearts? I reflect on how I would tell my 6-year-old daughter that we would have to leave our home simply because I became unhappy, or because I had a hard time feeding her. If I had my parents offering their hand, would I take it? Or would my pride win?

I am not angry at my parents, nor do I want you to be. I am not here to paint anyone as the villain. I am just here to share the truth, and it is not always pleasant. Even so, the truth habitually unveils its elegance and divine orchestration in one way or another, without exception.

I was always a storyteller. I think that my first demon appeared as I began to tell stories, because my style was not ever guileless. I quickly learned the artform of exaggeration and of stretching the truth.

I repeated the events and details of my father's absence over and over again to whomever would listen. My siblings and I would gossip about it: "What an asshole, I can't talk to him at all." We loved the drama.

It started shortly after his last visit, when we realized there was a side to be chosen: Mom or Dad. My dad was angry, and he was not afraid to express it. I was 9 or 10 when he began directing an accusatory tone toward my mother during his phone calls. He would tell us that my mom was in a cult, and he would try to diminish her parenting skills because she had started going to regular 12-step meetings. I was at the age where I understood a lot more, so his actions were an issue for me. I started hanging up on him or avoiding his calls.

He **was** the villain in my story for a long time. But I also felt sorry for him. I pictured him alone in that house, with a bottle in his hand, waiting for his family to return to him. That image always choked me up, and I felt guilty for not trying harder to stay close to him.

What I know now – and what I intend to write completely and truthfully – is that there were **many** pictures that got painted for me: they were painted by society, therapists, my grandparents, siblings, movies, and, of course, my own parents. A part of me knew that my father did not want to just be rid of us, like I often imagined. He was in pain. I now have a deeper and more compassionate understanding of human beings, and the ways they tend to their torments.

As a young girl, though, I checked out of the relationship with my dad. I shelved it in the hope that, one day, it would make sense to me. To be honest, it still does not. But I have released the need for answers or clarification. Today, I just love him, forgive him, and honor his journey.

Nobody is to blame. Both of my parents were young, and were healing wounds of their own – wounds from **their** childhoods, and from traumas inflicted on them by **their** parents. They continued a vicious ancestral cycle – one that I intend to dissolve before I die.

My dad and me, Israel

For my mother, 12-step programs were a safe haven. The people in the programs formed a community that became her family. She had a sponsor that called and held her accountable, and she had fellow alcoholics who helped her through her rage and supported her as a single mother of four.

Alcoholism was not necessarily her problem. She had an addictive personality complex that

olutely detested fasting. I also didn't like
at stopped me from turning on a goddamn
tch on a certain day of the week, and the rent for "modest" clothing. The clothes they
me to wear felt extremely unpleasant on my
lt like I was melting under the weight and
e fabrics, especially during summer.
g women were expected to dress the part
d little Jewish girl" in that town. We were
ved to expose our knees, our elbows, or our
es. Depending on the sector of Judaism,
rls were not even allowed to show their
his lifestyle was a major difference from
ad known before. We had always been
but it never felt like a rule that needed to
ed, "or else." After seeing that hot red one-
that lifeguard at my grandparents' place, I
rules even more. They seemed to force me
m expression and freedom. When I saw
people" outside our home or community,
feel the pang of envy. They were so **cool**,

those 12-step rooms helped her navigate. I do not remember her having a drinking problem, and she even later admitted that alcohol was not really the issue. Those rooms were a place where she could connect with other people in pain – others who were also healing from something that had a dangerous grip on them. Some were there because of the drink, others because of a needle or a pill. Some, like my mother, essentially were there because no other room on the planet understood her suffering quite as well.

My mother believed that the 12-step program she followed could benefit all humans. The fourth step in the program, "Make a searching and fearless moral inventory of ourselves," and the eighth step, "Make a list of all persons we have harmed, and become willing to make amends to them all," are examples how the program guides individuals toward personal growth and a spiritual path. The program was her medicine, and where her true mending began.

She actively participated in weekly meetings for about 10 years, and we met a lot of her friends from those rooms. Sometimes they would babysit or pick us up from school. If there was a youth-friendly event occurring, we would get to experience the energy of a healing community alongside her.

Years later, when my mother found her calling in the world of personal growth, she left the program with deep gratitude. She then moved on to workshops and interactions that specifically focused on healing root causes of depression, such as scarcity and rage. She connected and worked with many life coaches, and began her own practice of healing others through intuitive body work and empowering guidance. She also volunteered at the same workshops that she had attended for many years.

Today, since finding her groove, she might even have a glass of wine or two – with no shame.

Religion is for people who fear hell.
Spirituality is for people who have been there.
　　　　　　　　　　- David Bowie

I was inherently rebellious, and the first time I wore short sleeves outside of the house, there was hell to pay. Certain families shunned mine, and little minions pointed at me and whispered.

My closest friends were Demi and Mira. Demi was an American Israeli, which means that she was born in America, but her parents were Israeli. When she was at home, she was in an imaginary Israeli bubble. Hebrew was spoken, and Israeli meals were cooked. I sometimes felt **less** Israeli than her, because we did not speak any Hebrew at home once we left Israel. And, since my parents were American, there was a lack of true Israeli essence that Demi's family visibly had. They were darker-skinned as well, making them all the more "real life" Israelis.

I could feel the difference. It was obvious to me at that age that it was cool to be foreign, and I hated that I didn't have knowledge of my true heritage. About that time, I started lying to people about when I really arrived in the States.

I later learned that I am part Sicilian, Turkish, and Irish, as well as Russian, Polish, Austrian – just a good ol' mutt. And, my dad was adopted, but he did not find that out until he was in his 40's. I believe that not knowing where I was really "from" played a major part in my confusion. I felt like a lost duck.

Demi was my first true friend in America, and our friendship lasted until we were 12. She introduced me to her other Israeli friends. Adam, I remember vividly – he was in our second-grade class. He was my first hard crush. He had dark skin, too, with dark hair, chubby cheeks, and eyes as black as an abyss.

Oddly, Mira was the opposite. She was as tall and thin as a bamboo tree, with pale skin and hazel-green eyes. Though she was thin, she had wide hips and large breasts, giving her the hourglass shape of a woman at a young age. We were alike in that way. The difference was that she had a leveled belly; but to me, mine looked like the engorged risen dough for challah bread that my mother would bake for Shabbat.

I wondered about the difference between our bodies; it was one of the first times that I tilted my head with curiosity.

Mira had moved to Monsey from a preppy New Jersey area after her mother died from cancer and her father remarried. She was, naturally, very affected by her mother's death; but she still was always vibrant and playful. She is the fun and joy in many of my memories.

Mira's house was the first mansion I had ever seen. Now, as an adult, I know that it was just a suburban four-bedroom house with an updated kitchen and a two-car garage – hefty with some flash, but not a mansion. Her dad was a lawyer, and her stepmother was the county judge.

Demi and Mira helped me blend and become. My personality was forming alongside them during that crucial time. We had endless inside jokes that shaped my humor, and we three faced the religious world side by side, covertly resenting every second of it. They taught me the ropes, you could say.

Mira and I shared a kinship over rebellion and song. In the meantime, Demi and I played dress-up with her older sister's clothes, wrote fictional tales to each other – tapping into our infinite creativity – and built imaginary lives with her Barbie and Ken dolls. I spent a lot of time at both of their houses, especially because I liked how much more they had – more space, more food, more toys, more shine.

Demi showed me what sex was. She had recently seen her older sister having sex with a boyfriend, and took it as a learning opportunity. She grabbed my hand after class one day and pulled me into the bathroom. With one foot up on the toilet, she used her hand to imply where "it" goes in. I was so confused, yet so fascinated.

The majority of the town lived by its own rules, regulations, and committees. It was only one small section in a county of almost 40 cities; I would live in roughly 15 of them over the course of 10 years.

Down the road from Monsey, if you took Route 59, the main route that connected most of the county, you would find a primarily Hispanic area, with gang violence, drugs, and poverty. There used to be a tasteless running joke between neighbors in Monsey: "What's the quickest route from Israel to Mexico? Route 59."

My mother was a renter; and for a long time, we lived in places way too run-down to ever sign a

*Yearbook picture at one of the first schools
I attended in Monsey, New York*

second-year lease (the main reason we danced all over the county). To be fair, though, each place we rented did get better. We had three-bedroom homes that even had their own driveways by the end of our time in New York.

My mother was – and still is – an exceptionally uninhibited and powerful woman. She worked multiple jobs at once, and was unwaveringly devoted to seeing her way out of poverty, which she did. Along the way, she mastered and became certified in different modalities of health and fitness, which fit her calling of helping people heal and transform. My mother was equally committed to being a witness to all of her children growing healthy – not just alive, but thriving. Still, over the years, she would see two of us on the verge of death more times than she wanted to count.

While I was growing up, I observed that my friends, classmates, and surrounding neighbors were completely financially stable. We, on the other hand, appeared to be the only charity case. Some Fridays, before Shabbat, there were anonymous boxes left at our front door. They came from a non-profit organization tied to our local synagogue.

The boxes were filled with foods my mother would never be able to afford. In fact, she would not have even wanted to buy them, because they included many processed ingredients. She avoided those kinds of foods in her own grocery shopping and cooking. After a while, my mother finally asked the organization to stop sending the donated food.

The boxes of donated food had much heavier items than what our fridge usually held. There were things like bread baked with traditional white flour, and juices saturated with artificial flavors. But the boxes of food were always exciting for me, and I could not wait to sift through them when no one was looking.

I developed a food addiction at a young age and started hiding my habits early on. I would sneak into the kitchen at night and eat until my stomach felt like it was going to erupt. Much later, I learned what bulimia was. I was never a successful anorexic, since I loved food too much. I was absolutely stoked to find out that I could enjoy the food and then simply puke it up.

I felt the scarcity in our day-to-day life when I was in school, too. My classmates always had brand-new backpacks with their favorite cartoon characters and Disney princesses on them – with matching notebooks, lunch boxes and marker sets. They almost always had brownies with sprinkles in those lunch boxes, too.

Around that time, I met my kleptomaniac side. I would steal classmates' brownies during recess if I was able to sneak into the closet where we all kept our backpacks.

I do not know if I ever had a justifiable reason for stealing. I think it was simply a weakness and an envy that bypassed the thought process. I remember feeling terrified of being caught because I was aware of the wrongdoing.

My teen years were filled with theft. I would steal heaps of clothes from department stores, jewelry from little shops, and snacks from small grocery stores. I got so used to it – and became so comfortable with the act – that it was a given that when I walked into a store, I would walk out with something I did not pay for.

I finally got caught by an undercover security guard when I was 20. I actually put earrings in my ear from right off the shelf as I browsed. *Careless.*

I was banned from that department store for 10 years, with a $1000 penalty. I have not stolen anything since.

Most of the students in my school paid their tuition in full – from their own bank accounts, not from grants or financial aid like we did. They always received eight or more gifts on the famous eight-day Jewish holiday, Hanukkah. They collected iPods, brand-new Uggs, vacations, Juicy Couture – the works. My siblings and I were lucky if we were given one gift for the holiday, and it was usually something very small and very cheap.

Some years, my mother would just sit us down and tell us that she could not do anything at all. We always knew that she did her best; we never needed that shit anyway.

I lied every time that anyone asked about how old I was when we migrated to the US. Once I was in my mid-teens, the lie grew and I started saying I had been 12 when I came to the States (I was actually only 6). I thought that made me way more interesting, and the aghast reactions only added fuel to my desire to embellish my story.

For as far back as I can remember, I have detested the idea of looking or acting like everyone else. My innermost self always had the hunch that I was placed on this Earth for something big and purposeful. It felt heavy to know that. And when I was too young to understand or foresee what my "big" actually was, I tried to force the issue and create it in any way I could.

I would engineer a reason for people to look at me or listen to me just a little longer. I would attempt to sway and intensify their intrigue, even if it was just a facade. *Maybe,* I thought, *someone will recognize the vigor inside me, the usefulness, and the ache stemming from the unexpressed potential.*

Maybe they would save me from this life that did not feel like mine.

When this anticipation started, it devastated me. I was trapped in this little girl's body, but I had infinite waves of passion moving about inside, crashing up against the unbreakable walls of my skin, and unable to spread them to their full sweep.

I would look in the mirror with intense focus, thinking something might suddenly spill out, or show itself. I did not recognize the pigmentation, the body, or the life I was given.

I could have sworn I was dropped off at the wrong stop. Something more was meant for me.

I soon made a decision – an unconscious one – to descend, to dive, into the trenches of obscure and hazardous living. I wanted to see if I would find something there worth bringing back up to the surface of my god-forsaken reality.

I needed to find something, anything, that might lead me onto a path of grandiose and colossal living. I was unwaveringly sure that I belonged on such a path.

That unconscious decision stayed with me everywhere I went for years, and it wove its way into the crevices of my being. All of my eccentric and distinguishable personalities and lives were – in their essence – about finding my place. I sought a place where I could express, be, and belong – yet, move about without any constraints

Nothing fit right, nothing felt true.

In trying to step into my greatness and find my answers, I completely lost it. I became unrecognizable to myself, and to the people who raised me and grew up next to me.

I was 11 when I met my first love.

I was still in a private Jewish school (also called Yeshiva) and having even a little crush on someone was not something that was discussed, let alone accepted.

Being raised as a religious Jew only added to my feeling that I was born into the wrong life, but something inside me seemed already familiar with romance and a man's desiring gaze.

I ached for it.

I met Noah just after I turned 11 years old.

He was fairly tall, thin yet athletic, and had brown hair and brown eyes. His smile was wide, and he was a goofball. He was about two years older than I was, and my crush quickly grew to something more.

I remember making sure that his friend told him I was 11 now, not 10.

"I'm not a little kid anymore; make sure he knows it," I made sure to say, confidently.

This is absolutely comical now – granted, I **was** a little girl, but somehow I thought otherwise.

Noah and I would hang out at the mall. I was allowed a couple hours of alone time there if my mom was in a store across the way. Sometimes, I was permitted to go to a movie with friends, if there was some sort of adult supervision and a curfew. We had friends who were 18 and 21, so we would lie and say that someone's older sibling was supervising us. These older friends would even talk to my mom and play along if she needed proof. We would sneak into R-rated movies and make out quietly in the nosebleed seats. I was drinking and smoking weed regularly.

When I got sent to an all-girls sleep-away camp as punishment for my disobedience that summer, Noah and I would write letters to each other and count the days until my return.

I was soon kicked out of the camp for defiant behavior – ignoring the dress code and sneaking out past curfew to call Noah on the counselors-only pay phone.

I **wanted** to get kicked out. I absolutely hated every rule and every waking moment there. Being young and in love, or whatever it was, made it all the more appealing to get the boot. I was glad to be going home, although I did not hear the end of it from my mother.

After I was back home from camp, my relationship with Noah deepened.

The situation at his house was perplexing to me. There was no effective adult guidance. Noah and his siblings raised hell there, cursing and running free without consequences. They had an entire basement to themselves, where they threw parties, smoked, and played beer pong on a regular basis.

Some years later, I found out that it was in that basement where my little brother got high for the first time. His early experiences there led him into 10 years of drug addiction, juvenile detention centers, rehabs, and close calls with death.

Noah's folks, unaware and upstairs, dressed as traditional Jews and kept the holy Sabbath every week. Everything was kosher.

My family and I were the polar opposite – we were broke hippies from Israel who ran barefoot in the unpaved streets; we played musical instruments and made flower crowns. Noah's folks were people who worked in corporations and had 401k's. They had their own garages and mortgages.

Considering that my time spent at Noah's house was when I was between 11 and 14, I was deeply jealous of how free they were to do as they pleased. My mother was extremely strict, and she most definitely knew what it looked like when I was high.

A desire for freedom was the common thread in my youth. I wanted freedom from the constraints of my own skin; freedom from financial burdens and hearing the words "no, we can't afford that" every time I desired something. I wanted freedom to wear what I pleased. I wanted to run down the street and kiss the love of my romanticized life without feeling a heavy, invisible leash pull me back to stop my breath.

Please let me breathe, was all I ever thought.

It was not too long before my mother caught on to what she considered highly inappropriate behavior and settings for kids of our age. She was the type that needed to meet the other child's parents if her daughter was spending a lot of time at their house. It started becoming a huge problem to hang out there, or with Noah at all.

But I was in love, and there was no way I was staying away from him. The relationship with my mother became more strained and rage-filled as I ran away regularly to be with Noah. I wore black eyeliner, screamed into my pillow a lot, listened to hard rock, and only got

higher,

and higher,

and higher.

I frequently escaped through fantasy during this time. I would daydream for hours about being a famous singer with millions of dollars, saving my family from poverty.

As I write this, I am rolling my eyes at myself. *We all had this fantasy, right?*

Monsey, 2004

I reveled in the triumphant emotions that coursed through my body as I imagined being the hero in my own story. Influences like Christina Aguilera and Avril Lavigne were part of my everyday reverie. I knew every word to all of their songs, and I would mold my voice to theirs – melting into their stories, slipping away from my own.

This is partly why it took me so long to hear my own true voice. I was trying to sound like someone else for a long time.

I was barely 13 when Noah and I had sex for the first time. I quiver at the thought of my future daughter sleeping with someone at that age, but at the time, it felt so – right.

At the ages of 9 and 10 I had already encountered sexual incidents that led me to be more knowledgeable and prepared than I think I should have been.

My step-cousin Diana and I explored each other in the closet – twice. And since Demi had shown me "where the magic happens" in the bathroom the year before, I thought that knowing about it meant that I was ready.

My good friend Lauren and I had also explored one day after school. We stole her mom's thongs and felt each other out in the same way as Diana and I did.

I find it interesting, as a heterosexual woman, that my first sexual experiences were with women.

When I was 10 years old, I was at a small Jewish wedding when a drunk man in his 40s cornered me in a side room with glaring eyes and slurring his words. I remember being confused and slightly afraid. Before anything could happen, another adult witnessed the situation. She grabbed him and had him escorted out. She then took me to get some cake, helping me with sweets and a smile to forget about what might have happened, if she had not intervened.

Aside from those experiences forming some knowledge about sexual energy, Noah and I also had done our porn research. He learned from his older brother.

All of that previous information and experience combined, provided – in truth – not much more than just a slight understanding of what I was about to do.

We did not have a condom, and my first reaction to that obstacle was, "Oh well, it's just not the right time. We'll wait." But Noah was ready, and determined to find a solution.

It was 2 a.m. on a Saturday night, one of the nights that I had snuck over to his house, and it was completely quiet. Noah stormed around, looking for something we could use.

He came back with a sandwich bag. The kind that – thank God – did not have the green "zip." It was just thin, plastic film. He held it up with a shrug, as if to say, "Eh? Whaddya think?"

I agreed. He put some lotion on the bag – and slowly entered. Like it was yesterday, I remember the crinkling sound that the bag made, followed by a sonic "pop" that made me screech.

I ran to the bathroom, under the fluorescent light, to look at the blood that I knew had spilled out of me. Noah leaned on the door and watched me carefully. I thought we were done, considering the blood, but he wanted more. "I'm not done with you!" he said. "Come on, let's go back to bed." I submissively followed him, and began the journey of learning to give my body over for pleasure.

Noah and I had sex a lot. Once we got the hang of it, we were regulars. We would start with a condom, but very early on, I found that I hated them.

They seemed to only diminish the experience, and I already was not feeling much, or completely understanding the fascination that people had with the act.

During an argument with Noah that lasted a couple of weeks, a mutual friend mentioned that they had overheard him saying that having sex with me was like having sex with a wall or a dead fish. That made me angry. I decided I was going to be the best that he or anyone had ever had. I watched a lot of porn, and actively looked for ways to be worthier.

Watching porn helped me figure out what I was supposed to look and sound like. Little moans, a slightly opened mouth, lip biting, and putting on the marvelous show of **wanting it so badly.**

I was 13-and-a-half when things started taking a turn. My mother had officially enrolled us in public school, and things were different there. It is where I came to understand what I **looked** like, and what that meant.

It was the first time that I found out I was "sexy," a word I had never been called until leaving Yeshiva.

I found myself under the spell of the "cool kids" fairly quickly. During my first week, my natural instinct had been to sit with the "weirdos," because I felt like I belonged with them. I did not know yet about sects of "cool" or "nerdy" – only sects of Judaism. So, sitting at lunch with the ones who were a little goofy – the kids who had dandruff and ate their boogers – did not feel odd, until I was called out.

In my first-period class one day, I got a tap on my shoulder and a note was passed to me. I looked around and saw twin sisters synchronistically waving at me. I opened the note and all it said was, "Stop sitting with those losers, you're too pretty. Come to our table at lunch today."

It was middle-school Gossip Girl action, and I took the bait.

Cami came shortly after the twins, and she was a special kind of crazy.

On her mother's side, she was a fiery Puerto Rican – and on her father's, a white-as-light Jew.

Cami is, to date, one of the most beautiful girls I have ever seen. She has long, silky brown hair – the kind of hair that is perfectly straight and sleek as soon as it dries right out of the shower. It fell down to her perfectly-shaped peach-butt.

She was thick in the right ways, and her lips were so full and defined that Angelina Jolie might snarl if she walked by her. To top it off, her blue eyes could pierce right through you, and she made sure that they did.

Cami was a savage, to say the least. We met in eighth grade, when we were both at the end of our 13th year, and at the height of our mischievous behavior. Trouble was our middle name, and we loved every second of it. She took me under her wing fairly quickly, and we were completely inseparable. We ate lunch together, flirted with the boys, cut class, got high after school (or during), went to the junior and senior parties, and had regular sleepovers.

There was an unspoken jealousy, too. We both knew that when a boy was standing in front of us, he would have a hard time picking his favorite.

Cami loved to flaunt her spitefulness. If a girl pissed her off or crossed her in any way, she would say things like, "Fuck me over, and I'll fuck your boyfriend – or your dad, and I'll make you my stepdaughter." I have no idea where she got that content. But she was cold.

The difference between Cami and I was that she **loved** being the mean girl. It was a persona she used at random. She would announce proudly, "I eat boys for breakfast." She had a sarcastic evil laugh that made me twitch. She was not afraid to roll her eyes at you, blow you off, or shove you into a locker and walk away laughing.

Once, she straddled me in my bedroom and pierced my belly button. We were out of our minds. That piercing became extremely infected, and got ripped out some time later. The scar remains visible today, a brutal reminder of the disaster I allowed on my body.

Cami taught me (at 14) that I was never to answer a boy's text after 10 p.m., and that if he texted me during the day, I needed to wait a few hours in order to "play the game" before responding to him.

We were different in that way. I was a double-texter if I was ignored by a boy, and I was called annoying many times.

I had a soft spot for the boys Cami bullied. There was one – Dave – who reminded me of that little boy from pre-school in Israel. He was your typical Type A nerd. He played the trombone, wore his backpack as high up on his shoulders as he could get it, and had New Balance sneakers with socks up to mid-calf. Cami tried to shove him into a locker a few times.

My chest burned at her behavior, but I still followed her. I admit it – I was slightly afraid, because she could and **would** hurt me.

My corrupt new friends and growing substance abuse – along with receiving a whole lot of new attention – led me to start lying to Noah about talking to other boys and partying with the public-school students. I also broke promises we had made, like the one to never tell anyone we were having sex, which was important to him. He finally ended it with me.

I was devastated to the core. To this day, I can remember what it felt like when he made it clear that he was really done. I knew it, because when I called and texted him, he completely ignored me.

We are still friends, and when we recently talked about that moment in our history, he said it was the hardest thing he had ever done. He was a young boy, and did not know how to handle a breakup. So – he Googled, "How do you break up with someone?" and the results told him to ignore the person at all costs.

It was the only time I recall truly feeling my heart **break.**

Every painful experience following that one would never compare to the ache I felt at losing my first love.

I remember being bent over on the ground, holding my chest and stomach, silently screaming, with tears flooding my face as I lay on the floor. I had never known anything like it. The pain felt like flames burning up my insides, and I physically could not breathe.

I felt abandoned, chucked aside, lifeless.

At times, I would breathe through my nose in the middle of a deep cry. It felt as though a wave swallowed me unexpectedly and a load of salt water was ingested. I was coughing, gasping, the veins in my neck engorged. It reminded me that I was grateful to be alive.

A little while after our breakup, Noah started openly dating a new girl. I had been distracted by getting drunk and high with my friends and making out with junior and senior boys.

The pain of losing and loving him was still there; I was just slapping a bad habit Band-Aid on it. At night, I was crying into my pillow.

Through the grapevine, I heard someone say, "Noah says Sarah has a prettier face, but his new girlfriend has a way better body."

There it was.

That was the comment that made me look at myself every day for years and conclude that I was not good enough.

That this body is garbage.

That somebody better throw me out before I do.

I held scissors to my belly fat, I cut my wrists, I threw up my food, and I got very wasted – often.

I sink deeper into the memory. Before that comment was made, I did not have a disturbing hatred for my physical body.

Why did that comment have such an impact on me? Was that remark really what did it, or were there other critical things happening along with it – or before it – that I did not consciously process?

Maybe that comment was just the thing that put me over the edge – or gave me a dark green light to delve deeper into the self-hatred that I was already manifesting. Maybe I just needed an excuse – a story for my story.

There, right THERE, is why I am so fucked up.

Many of us – or at least the ones trying to understand why we are the way we are – the ones spending our lives trying to heal it all – often return to the places where the damage was done. We analyze and point at the traumas that might equate to the reasons why we turned out a certain way.

Maybe it is not possible to point at one thing, or even two, that did the breaking. Maybe it is not even from this lifetime. And maybe we just need to let it go.

For our 10th-grade pep rally, I met up with my girls at Amy's house. Amy was a wild one, and her mother never gave a shit what we did, so we would always go over there to be bad.

We were "pregaming" for the pep rally; Apple Bacardi shots were passed around before we headed over to the school.

Shannon, another in our group of unruly teens, was drunk while driving. We blasted pop rock from the wide open windows, sticking our heads and hands out, letting the wind kiss our cheeks, while we sang along to the words of "Young, Wild & Free."

I had absolutely no limits, and I was chugging Bacardi from the bottle. *Fuck it* might as well have been plastered on my forehead.

We arrived late.

The doors to the gymnasium were closed and I was fucking belligerent. I actually walked face first into the door.

Blackout.

> *sometimes*
> *the whole world of women*
> *seems a landscape of*
> *red blood and things*
> *that need healing*
> – Lucille Clifton

I woke up in the hospital.

"I want to die. Please let me die," I said.

My mother was holding my hand.

I laid there – confined, next to a bedpan – with alcohol poisoning. They told me that an ambulance took me from the principal's office after a security guard witnessed me walking into the door.

Noah was the only thing on my mind; and when I tried to get up, they held me down and told me I had to stay. Tears poured out of me, and I asked no one in particular why he did not want me. I kept repeating that I wanted to die.

What happened next is fuzzy, but it was decided that I needed help.

I was involuntarily taken to an inpatient rehabilitation center called FW.

Interestingly, at the front door, I ran into Mira, my childhood friend. She was checking in as well, with her dad by her side.

We laughed together at the hilarity of the situation – running into each other after years of not staying in touch, remembering our wild ways as kids, and then meeting again at a place for troubled teens on the same day.

Synchronistic.

I spent two weeks at FW. My days consisted of therapy, group exercises, breakfast, lunch, and dinner. In one therapy session, with the facility's psychiatrist, I was prescribed Prozac. It was my first medication for major depressive disorder.

"We're going to try different cocktails until the right one sticks. It's a process, but have faith," the psychiatrist told me. I remember being terrified of gaining weight.

After the first week, they upped my dose.

I do not remember that it helped me, though my mother says when I was consistent in taking it, she saw enormous differences in my personality.

I fake-swallowed and spit it out, usually.

I made friends with one of the girls there, Gina, who was quite literally the coolest chick I had ever met. There was just something about her – she was Dominican, and born and raised in Brooklyn. Her personality was "Queen B" energy, but she was humble and kind too.

I remember her laugh, her spicy attitude, and little body. She was short and petite; she had curly brown hair with the most perfect slicked edges, and little – yet shapely – soft lips.

She made it easier for me to be there by making me smile a lot. She also taught me how to twerk – gleefully and with encouragement, she launched "Operation: Help Sarah Shake Her Big Booty."

I was always an awkward thing when it came to movement. Although my hips should have inherently had a rhythmical flow due to their extraordinary shape and size, the disassociation that I felt to my body never allowed me to catch a beat gracefully.

We ate our meals and went to the mandatory groups. We "took" the mandatory medications and did our mandatory one-on-one therapy sessions. I counted the days until I would be free.

It was Gina who taught me how to carry myself in that facility; and it is a good thing that she did, because I would end up spending a great deal of the following years in and out of similar places.

It was always the strangest feeling to leave any rehab facility after weeks or months, and to walk outside into the daylight. I would walk out with my mother, usually holding a plastic bag filled with my few belongings. I would look around, perplexed. It sort of felt like waking from a coma.

What did I miss? Did anyone ask about me? Everything seemed quite outlandish. The world always carried on while I was absent.

For my second time in treatment, I was admitted into the psychiatric unit of a larger hospital in the tri-state area. Where I had been taken before – FW – was mostly a combination of drug addicts and kids who were just constantly getting high with their friends. I think that our behavior frightened our parents and they just did not know what to do with us.

The psychiatric unit of a major hospital was a little more extreme. It was not considered drug rehab at all, but was more for serious "chemical imbalances": schizophrenia, bipolar disorder, eating disorders, major depressive disorder – things like that.

I dragged my feet as my mother brought me into the hospital at 7 a.m. My eyes were heavy from days of crying and with black eyeliner. I compulsively pulled at my pierced lip with my teeth.

I couldn't tell you what I did that particular time that justified my need for rehab, since events from those years are all blurred together. Sometimes it was getting high, sometimes it was cutting my wrists, or throwing up my food, or it was an aggressive and manic episode where I lost it on everybody. Sometimes, I ran away – but I always got caught. I cannot tell you "which" was "when."

There was a lot of waiting time in those facilities. There were waiting rooms with worried, naive parents and disgusting black coffee. Their angry, jittery teens would sit beside them, their body language saying, "Stay away, or else." Two-year-old magazines would be scattered nearby on torn-up chairs. Inevitably, emerging young artists who happened to be in rehab slashed graffiti into the furniture's arms and seats.

My heartbeat accelerates as I reminisce about those rooms; I was in them an indeterminate number of times. I feel like a fly on the wall now, scanning the scene in my memory. I am trying to understand what was happening then. I watch my younger self walk into the bathroom as my mother discusses my diagnoses with the doctors.

"Unstable... danger to herself and others... high risk... unpredictable... need to up her medication... suicidal."

I search the bathroom for a way to escape, but there is nothing. Instead, I nonsensically pull an earring out of my ear and place it on the counter. I look at the earring, then look in the mirror. My eyes are bloodshot-red, and when I see my reflection, I feel the anger at my own face ascend up from my belly into my chest. I run to the toilet and stick my fingers all the way down my throat for a release of energy, hoping the emotional disgust is something I can puke up. I walk back to the mirror and stick my tongue out again, but this time to pierce it with the small earring. It hurts, but not any worse than the sting I felt when I looked in the mirror.

I come out of the bathroom and plop myself on the couch when I am asked to join the conversation about my treatment.

"Bipolar II... going to start her on Latuda... mood stabilizers... we're going to keep her for a few weeks," I hear the doctor saying.

> **Bipolar II disorder**
> A type of bipolar disorder characterized by depressive and hypomanic episodes. It involves at least one depressive episode lasting at least two weeks and at least one hypomanic episode lasting at least four days.

I feel drunk, numb. I do not care about anything. My tongue is throbbing.

I found myself standing in the hallway of a psychiatric unit – **again.**

I was thrown in with a group of kids from all over New York and New Jersey. Some were from Harlem and the Bronx, some were from Paterson, some were from White Plains.

It was late afternoon. We had been told to go to our rooms for "quiet time" before our evening group; but on that day, I chose not to move.

I was vaguely aware that it was raining. My mind could get lost in suicidal ideation, and while I listened to the rain, I couldn't help but wonder what it would be like to fucking drown.

They didn't know it, but the night before, I had tried to kill myself. If you had asked me about it then, I would have said that it was funny how it happened. After the lights went out, a guard sat by our bathroom. The bathroom had a pink door and checkered floors, and the guard stayed there all night to make sure no one went in for longer than three minutes. Suicide attempts were common – we were monitored in every way possible.

Windows were barred. Knives were not allowed in the cafeteria, which meant that we buttered our toast with a spoon. And if you wanted to shave your legs, you had to set an appointment with one of the nurses to oversee your every razor stroke.

During my intake processing, where they remove all your jewelry and do a full-body and personal-belongings search, the staff overlooked the string that wrapped around my journal to keep it shut. Somehow, I made it into the bathroom while the guard went to grab another cup of coffee. She must have hoped that it would keep her up and alert for the overnight shift.

In the bathroom, I unwrapped the long string from my journal and bound it tightly around my neck. I pulled and pulled, but nothing happened. I was choking – but only from crying so hard.

I don't know if I was in that bathroom for 10 minutes or three hours; but I lay on that checkered floor with my tears streaming for what seemed like days. I fought for a breath every few seconds, feeling more pathetic than I ever had.

When I walked out with my tail between my legs and my neck as red as a ready pimple, the guard shot up out of her seat.

"What the **fuck?** I had no idea anyone was in there. Are you **insane?** Go to your room, **now.**"

I had nothing left in me for a response or a fight. I walked slowly to my room and lay awake the rest of the night, wondering, *Why does it never work?*

Like any teenager, I was tired of being told what to do. Tired of being sent to my room. Tired of being treated like a prisoner. Tired of having no say.

So as I battled with myself the following day during that rainy afternoon, I just stood there after being instructed to go to my room.

Fuck it.

A counselor walked toward me with determined footsteps. A few of the counselors were good with the kids there, but he was not one of them. He was staring me down. On the outside, I put up a hard front, even though I had no idea how it would go for me. I had seen counselors react to challenges with wild measures, so anything could happen.

But I was numb, pumped with medications that I did not want in me, and I wanted to stir shit up. My spirit was aching for something that felt alive.

"Miss Becker," he said firmly, "go to your room!"

My eyes glazed over. I did not have a plan.

He repeated again, "Go to your room now."

I didn't move.

"Sarah." The counselor's voice became threatening. "I said now."

Stay, I told myself. *You don't have to move, you don't have to do anything.*

"MISS, DO YOU HEAR ME?"

What should I do? I thought. I was standing my ground, but my feet started to feel like they had unintentionally loitered in wet concrete overnight.

"Give me a minute," I said, head down, eyes locked on the floor. I could still hear the rain outside. It was a storm. Or maybe that was just the weather inside of my trapped fucking body.

Whichever one it was, the volume was full blast and my vision was pounding.

What I would give to be outside of this prison right now.

I flinched as the counselor grabbed my arm and tried to walk me to my room.

"You don't want to do this," he said, as I resisted. "Let's go."

I snatched my arm away, but he grabbed it harder and pulled me. We grappled for a bit before I ripped away. He came from behind and wrapped himself around me with both arms. I tried to slide through, and we both went to the ground.

Now it was a hospital emergency. On cue, the alarms went off throughout the ward.

Shit.

A nurse yelled for guards, and the next moments were complete chaos. Two guards ran to us, then another two, and then two more – because you need a half-dozen grown men to hold down a medicated 16-year-old girl. Right?

They wrestled me to the floor and held me down. The alarm kept blaring, filling my head with the noise. For a second, it felt like my lungs were closing. I screamed then – but the blaring of the alarm drowned out my voice.

Out of nowhere, the nurse pulled out a long needle and shot me up with a tranquilizer. I felt tremors go through my body before it went limp. With the nurse leading the way, the guards carried me to a padded room, arranged me on the bed, and strapped down my arms and legs.

I raged against the stillness. My body could not move and my mind felt scrambled, but I was not thinking in words. Wild images filled my brain; intense sensations and panic coursed through me. Visions of half-baked escape plans spun me deeper into turmoil. I couldn't move even an inch in any direction, but still I thrashed. I was livid and confused – completely disoriented.

They had my wrists and ankles strapped to navy blue pads that were soaked with my tears. I didn't even know I had been crying. It was not until later – while lying defeated on my back – that I noticed the wetness behind my ears, and felt the pool of my wet hair and the strands stuck on my face.

I was exhausted; my rage gave way to sadness and humiliation. The defeat was all-consuming. The feeling of wanting to leave was so overpowering I couldn't take it. My sadness became whiny, even – I was whimpering like a helpless animal.

I returned frequently to thoughts of escape; but realistically, I knew they were fantasies.

I felt imprisoned – not just physically, but existentially. My body was not mine. The sadness was too hard to endure – the despair too real. I was tapped out of rage and the only thing I could do was disassociate. So, I checked out.

In many ways, I spent much of the next 10 years living that way – on autopilot. I made choices that were not really mine, because I left the real me tied down on that bed. The panic I felt – the mindfuck of having no control – led me to **lose** control.

A few minutes after I was strapped down on the bed, my favorite counselor walked into the guarded room. I had been there frequently enough that she considered me a friend.

"Sarah?" she asked in surprise. "Is that you?"

I thought of what I probably looked like, lying there, and I was suddenly ashamed to have her see me like that.

"When I heard it was you, I couldn't believe my ears. I really thought you didn't belong here. What the hell happened?"

Fresh tears filled my eyes as I turned my face away. I silently wished the suicide attempt the night before had worked.

The counselor said she thought I didn't belong there. But it was not just "there" where I didn't feel that I belonged. I did not want to be anywhere.

I don't remember what we were fighting about. I was 16, and I was either just getting back from the hospital or on the verge of going back. It was around that time that I started having trouble with my memory. I was not only getting high and drunk frequently, but I was also on a prescribed cocktail of antidepressants and mood stabilizers. My mom and I were going back and forth about whatever it was I did wrong that time, and as our voices rose, I packed a backpack of my belongings – and ran.

The last time I had done that, I found myself in a young women's shelter, eating fried chicken and sleeping on half of a twin-size bed with six other homeless girls.

By the time I decided to run again, I had been placed in a small special education school about 15 minutes away from the main public school. They sent the troubled students there. The students' conditions ranged from severe depression and attention-deficit disorder to Tourette's syndrome and autism. I was in and out; when I did make it to class, I would mostly sleep.

With my life in chaos and nothing helping me, my mother could not handle the tornado that I brought home every day. Finally, she would not let me back in the house. The hospital, the shelter, rehab, or the streets were my choices.

A girlfriend offered to have me stay at her place, but I would need to pay her rent. I had no money, so that was out. I searched my mind for who to call.

Bob was the first person who came to mind.

I first met Bob when I was about 13. He was in his early 40s then. He was a good friend of my mom and became one of my favorite people. At that time, I hardly spoke to my dad and had no father figure in my life, other than my mother's occasional boyfriend.

But Bob was someone special to me. He radiated an engaged energy and joy that I wished my father had. Hearing that he would visit made me giddy; it was like Santa was coming. When I heard his name, I instantly sat up and my ears perked. "Bob's coming by?" I'd ask. And if he was, it was Christmas.

I could not really tell you what it was that started my enthrallment with him. Perhaps it was his obvious wealth and the fact that he was always in a suit. That easily fascinated my young, impoverished eyes. He was a wealthy businessman, and he would either come by on his motorcycle or in his convertible car. He also had an incredible sense of humor that would send me into belly laughs. No one was cooler. My siblings and I idolized him.

I remembered the words that he had spoken to me, more than once:

"If you ever need anything, I'm here."

So on that gray day, as I walked down the street with my bag, not a dollar on me, I phoned Bob. He told me to stop by his office.

I do not know what compelled me, but I took time to make myself a little more presentable before heading over. I was excited to see him.

I put on a red shirt that was a hand-me-down from my older sister, along with a dab of eyeliner and some lip gloss. I remember taking extra time with my wet hair, smoothing and accentuating the waves with my favorite hair mousse.

When I walked into his office, he gestured for me to take a seat across from him at his desk. We started catching up – I told him about my hospital visits and how much I hated school, and he told me about his fun life as a business owner. I told him that I was moving out on my own, and proceeded to ask if his offer to help me was still on the table.

"Absolutely. Just tell me how much you need," Bob said.

I gave him an amount that would cover half of the rent and some money for food. He wrote an $800 check and put it down on the desk. A wave of relief surged through me.

That relief vanished when, all of a sudden, he looked at me in a way that he never had before. I remember the shift in the air, as if the AC stopped running at that exact moment.

"God, you've gotten really fuckin' hot," he said as he cocked his head.

He came around the desk and leaned into me. I felt his hot breath as he came in for a wet kiss. My heart started pounding, and fear gushed through me like a bursting waterfall.

The office chair was the kind that moved back when weight was pressed into it, and I remember feeling like I was falling. I froze – and kissed him back – as I noted the check on the desk in my peripheral vision.

Something told me that if I stopped him, I would be back on the street without that check.

I never fought back; I never said no. I thought that going along was the way to protect myself from violence; and I held to that belief during many sexual encounters in the years following.

If I act like I want it, they can't hurt me.

Unbeknownst to me – and regardless of whether I said **yes** or **no** – the damage would be unavoidable. My body did **not** want that. Scars were left.

But the unspoken agreement between us began right there.

When he called, I came – and he supported me financially for many, many years.

The games he played disturbed me. He knew he owned me.

If I told him I could not make it to his office when he requested a visit, he would say things like, "Sorry, my bank isn't working today." And though I knew there was no such thing as the "bank not working," I pretended to be naive.

Then I would figure out a way to get to his office.

Sometimes our meetings would be after hours, on his desk; other times, they would be during the workday in the janitor's closet of his building.

I was still in high school.

Bob had gotten a vasectomy after having two sons with his ex-wife, so he finished inside of me every time. Whenever I left him, I was dripping with his dead seed. I would go numb.

My self-hatred grew **almost** irrevocably.

You know when you are on your way down a rollercoaster. There is that feeling – like your breath is lost for a millisecond, and then a dreadful panic takes over for an unaccounted amount of time – and it's almost like it didn't happen when it finally passes? That's what I felt every time I walked into Bob's office.

I felt it when I saw his name come up on my phone, and I felt it when the bare truth of what I was doing crept forward in my mind. Soon, though, I managed to bury those thoughts. I intended to take them to the grave.

There was an invisible chain that grew from the foot of Bob's desk, extended to me and was locked around the five inches of my wrist. And I had utterly no idea how to break it. My teenage mind only knew what programs were playing, along with the images and events of my tiny world. I did not yet know that I had a choice; that I did not have to do what Bob wanted me to do; that I had more to offer than my body; and that I was actively playing a part in, and contributing to, the suffering of my lineage. I was on ancestral autopilot, following in the footsteps of the ones who had come before me, confined in a loop of scarcity and unworthiness.

I played along with Bob, obediently, for 10 years – acutely aware of my role as his sex toy. I even said things like "I love you, I know you care about me," and gave him sweet, innocent smiles on my way out of his office.

I always held my tears until I was on the road.

His scent follows me around even today – a nauseating combination of a very specific cologne and the sweat that was trapped in the foreskin of his uncircumcised penis.

In my mind, I had to do everything in my power to hide the deep disgust that moved through me –

and was slowly devastating me – because of what I was doing.

That money from Bob kept me and my family fed, although they never knew where it came from.

The equally challenging and repulsive thing was that Bob had no idea I was anything other than a high school girl. He had no idea that I was in a relationship with someone else most of the time that I was involved with him.

And when I went home to my lover, I would wipe my feet and leave my dirty deeds at the door. I would then walk inside, externally unmarred, and say, "Hi baby, I'm home. Want me to make us some dinner?"

A parallel life.

I have agonized over what telling these parts of my story might do to my "reputation." So, how much did I really mean it when I said I would speak the whole truth, and was I serious when I vowed to share all of me to help others heal?

"Use me all up, God," was something I heard my mother pray once. She understood that her past was something gifted to her in order to help others. She ached for ways to be of service. I feel the same way.

Over the years, anytime I have revealed something of my life – whether in a whispered conversation in a public place, at the dinner table with my roommates, in a circle at a women's gathering, or simply on Instagram – someone would ask for more. Someone would say, "Please, share. I need (or, my sister, my daughter needs) to hear this."

It was validating to hear. But still, for a long time, fear won, and I could not bring myself to do it.

Ego would say to me, *"You are a slut and that is not a story. That is just a fact you'll be telling the world, opening the door for online trolls, notorious harassment, and cruel judgment. Are you addicted to punishing yourself?"*

That voice followed me around most of my life. It showed up at a young age and stuck around like an aggressive loiterer.

Julia was 27. We were both in 12-step programs at the time – for different reasons and with a significant age gap – but we still felt a kinship and connection that we could not explain at the time. Our liaison was a toxic one, although I genuinely loved her. She had a young son who had a heroin addict for a father and who constantly mistreated her. We chain-smoked and talked about hating our bodies and our monotonous lives. Nonetheless, we showed up for each other.

I was 15 when I started going to those 12-step meetings; they were usually mandatory for me since I was an outpatient from some of the hospitals and rehab places.

Sometimes I went just to please my mother; still, I do not remember ever really paying attention. I slept with a couple of men in their late 20s during my first few weeks at the meetings, and treated the follow-up gatherings as a place to see them again. The meetings were never about healing for me.

I just needed to be wanted and distracted, and each meeting room that I went to gave me more ammo for my goals.

I know that to be true on a much deeper level now. Why else did I go searching for men who were obviously inadvisable for me? These were **grown** men: addicts, living in their mother's basements, and usually on parole. And these were men who would sleep with a teen.

Why did I beg for their acknowledgement? And why was my body the thing that I threw at them, as if it was a steak being thrown to a hungry dog?

I think back to my father's "Mr. Cellophane" days. I was youthful – just blossoming – and a little girl. Yet, I was evidently vastly affected by his lack of attention in those years. Was it such a bruise to my psyche that I spent 15 years trying to find him in other men? Did a buried part of me resent the fact that he never stayed – that he never came back to get me?

I used to absolutely detest the "daddy issues" comments that were made by my peers during my adolescence. "I don't have daddy issues," I'd say. "My dad isn't even around to give me issues."

Undoubtedly, I did not know what "daddy issues" truly meant. Still, it is a far too shallow and indecent term to adequately describe the intricate ways that my father's absence influenced this young girl's mind.

I had just turned 17 when Julia and I went to a small pub in Jersey one night after our regular Sunday meeting.

I quickly locked eyes with the bartender. "**Who the fuck** is that?" I asked no one in particular, and without actually needing an answer.

James had messy hair with one long strand hanging down the back of his neck, and a feather intertwined – a rat tail, my mother called it. He was tattooed from the neck down, and had an irresistible look in his eye.

He was the image of a rockstar.

I fell so hard and fast for that delightful heroin addict. It was a potent, high-speed fall. I waited at the bar that night for him to close down around 4 a.m., and went home with him. Our first night together bound us for what I felt might be an eternity.

Back at his place, James concocted a meal. It was the first time a man had ever cooked for me. I decided that meant he was the one.

A man, actually taking care of me.

James prepared steaks on the grill for us, and even cut them into fine little pieces. Then, he tossed them into an extravagant salad – completing the marvelous performance.

I was enamored.

It was 5 a.m., and I had only known him for about seven hours, but that was enough for me.

James washed my body attentively in the shower, even getting down into a squat to reach the bottoms of my feet. And when we got out, he showed me how to fold the sleeves of my T-shirts in a way so that they would never roll down. He even taught me how to make a grilled cheese sandwich in a way that no one could deny its full flavor.

I always paid close attention to his little teachings, and I felt my gaze sharpen on him every time. Nothing excited me more than learning how to do things in a way that made me feel young and wide-eyed.

Things my father might have shown me if he had stayed.

I felt safe at the beginning. When we made love that first night, I breathed in deep pleasure and fell in love for a whole three minutes.

James was a musician with deferred dreams, working his way through his addictions and procrastinations. He was talented; an archetypical broken artist. He was a man with a guitar, an addiction, and little to his name – in other words, someone who could easily creep his way into the crux of my being.

> *Crux*
> *The most important point at issue; a particular point of difficulty; from the Latin - "cross, torture, trouble"*

We stayed together for about a year, on and off – and ebbing halfway through.

Our sex was dopey; he would almost always nod off in the middle. Even while going down on me, I would feel him recede and wither. I would jump up in disbelief when I realized he had drooped completely; it would scare both of us. "I'm sorry baby, it was a long shift tonight," he'd say. And I always believed him.

Around the same time that I found a needle in James's bathroom, I found an identical needle in my little brother's.

My brother Levi's story is not mine to tell, just as my grandmother's is not. But what **is** mine, is the love I have for him – and how the course of his life-threatening addiction weaved in with my own in a way I cannot fully explain.

My mother identified it.

"When he's in rehab, you're home. When he comes home, you're back in the hospital before I can even sit down to breathe. It's like you both wait for each other," she would point out. We are 22 months apart, and our journeys always found a way to meet along the way.

It started when we were younger, when I was about 13 and he was 11. We would come home past curfew, high as giraffe nuts, and look at each other – then, we'd burst out laughing. We always knew.

We started a ritual of late-night munchies in the kitchen, whispering, and hoping that we would not get caught. Sometimes we were, with my mom walking in, livid. She would hiss, "You're fucking high, aren't you?"

As unmanageable as we were, she never failed to scare the shit out of us.

I felt a deep, measureless love for my brother form around that time; it still pulsates through me.

I am just his big sister; but I think I was something else to him in another life, because sometimes it is as though we shared an umbilical cord. My concern for him is like that of a mother for her child.

Sometimes, to this day, I find myself in a rabbit hole of fear for him. I worry that something has happened to him, and I call him just to make sure he is alive. Other times, I start crying with gratitude, overwhelmed with joy that he is breathing and thriving today.

Simply put, I imprinted on him in a way that is beyond comprehension or definition.

With all of that summarized, I return to the day that I found James's needle.

It happened after months of watching his addiction worsen; I had consistently witnessed him taking different types of pills. He began nodding off more often. Sometimes he would borrow money from me, with no explanation. And then, as I became disenchanted by his drug use, I started falling for someone else. But more on that later.

One evening, I walked into the bathroom to take a shower and there it was – a syringe, just sitting there, like a hairbrush or a nail clipper or a Q-Tip on a vanity. It did not look elaborate or even particularly remarkable.

It had a thin, pointed needle, almost as thin as string, extending outward from a plastic tube. I knew what it was from movies and books, and conversations in rehabs. But it was my first time seeing one in person. It scared me to bits.

James denied it was his. He blamed his brother, who was staying with him after coming home from a year in prison. We left the conversation alone, though I knew well that he was lying. After all, I was an expert on that.

Later that night, James was watching a movie in the living room on a large recliner while his brother slept on the couch beside him. I had just come out to join them, and found myself spacing out while standing behind James' chair, lazily rubbing his shoulders. I remember the eeriness in the air, and the odd, quiet feeling. It was summer, and the front door in the kitchen was usually unlocked, with the screen door letting in the breeze.

I heard it slam but I did not budge, still in a daydream. I then felt a presence in the doorway of the living room; I slowly turned to my left. I was in complete disbelief of what I saw. My imagination would sometimes run wild and so I wondered for a moment if I was dreaming.

A man, taller than any I had ever seen before, stood with his head cocked far to the right. He was looking sideways, but right at me. He wore a face mask, with then-President Obama's features painted on. A knife was tucked into his waistband. It is not an image I have ever forgotten.

I was still so frozen in my body that I made no move when he scanned the room and jumped on James' brother, missionary-style. He began to crack his brother's face with his fists. James' large recliner chair was facing away from the entrance and the man did not know that James was in it. It all happened in about 20 seconds, and finally, I could move my fingers.

I tapped James' shoulder. He had nodded off.

"James," I whispered, "James… James!" My tap became a forceful hit on his shoulder, and I found my voice, breaking out of my seemingly frozen spell. James' brother, having been asleep, looked like a lifeless rag doll being pummeled into the couch. When James finally sprang up, he ripped the man off of his brother. Within moments, they were both fully awake, both attacking the man who had broken into their home.

They had not seen the knife yet, and I screamed hoarsely, "He has a knife in his pants!"

James saw it right then, and screamed back at me, "Lock yourself in the bathroom and call the police, now!" I ran to the bathroom with legs feeling like jelly; I fell to the floor in the corner, locking myself in like I had been told. My fingers shook violently as I dialed 911.

By the time the police arrived, the man was unrecognizable and sprawled out on the front lawn. James and his brother had beaten him so badly that his face was damaged and completely bloodied.

Shortly after the cops dragged the man into an ambulance, the truth surfaced. The boys had owed that man drug money.

I became very detached after that incident. I started working at a small ice cream shop, frequently running to the bathroom to scoop up cocaine from a baggie with my car key before scooping up Cotton Candy Swirl for customers.

I told James we were done, but he was adamant about keeping us together. He showed up to my work the day after the breakup, flashing his new tattoo of my face on his forearm. His thought process was: if he got a tattoo of my entire face, even after I broke up with him, there was no way I could really leave. I fell back in with him for a while, but it didn't last too much longer.

The job at the ice cream shop was short-lived. The owner was a crabby man – and my fiery attitude, mixed with cocaine, did not help the situation. But to be truthful, he **was** constantly belittling his workers and speaking to us disrespectfully. I shared a piece of my mind with him, and although he was understanding and apologetic, I quit right after. The pay was shit, and it was all a front anyway.

During that time, my mental stability was still very fragile.

Finally, I told on myself for the first time. Not directly – but when my mom picked me up on that notable night, it began a domino effect.

I knew that once she arrived, she would find out who exactly had registered for the hotel room.

I had been staying with James on and off, but on that night I had told him I was going away for a night or two to get some "me time."

In reality, Bob had insisted that I go to the Marriott, and directed me to wait for him in room 218.

When Bob left – about 20 minutes after he arrived – the emotions I had been routinely burying poured out of me. They were like a tsunami crashing through a small city.

Those emotions filled every pore, flipped my organs upside down, and created a physical feeling of terror far beyond what my body was prepared to hold.

The feeling stirred in my gut and pounded through my chest like a caged animal, desperate and violent to get out. It brought me to my knees.

The only option I thought I had was to take my own life. It was an option that had been casually sitting across from me for years – I saw an image in the mirror wearing a leather jacket, sporting black eyeliner, and smiling with a low glare, all the while twisting a knife masterfully into the reflection between us.

Sometimes I would reach for that knife, nonchalantly, as if I was reaching for the salt.

But every time I made an attempt to end my life, a force greater than myself would snatch the opportunity away.

That night at the hotel, I had more resolve. I took my last $1000 in cash, flushed it down the toilet, and proceeded to cut up my ID. The logic in all of that was that I meant serious business. *I am going to die and no one can stop me this time,* I thought.

I had a bottle of pills that would do the job.

But as soon as I was ready, I collapsed into victimhood, tears pouring out of me. In a fetal position with black makeup pouring down my face, I called my mother to come save me. And she did, like she always has.

Later, I found out that I had accidently given her the wrong address. She rushed out, only to knock on the door of room 218 of a different hotel entirely – finding someone who was not her daughter. Fearful that she would be too late, her panic escalated.

During those blurred years of hospitals, relapses and rehabs, my mother was as present as any parent could possibly be. On one hand, she was balancing the hospital visits and arrests of my little brother and trying to feed and protect my little sister. On the other hand, she was balancing my insanity with her own emotional challenges and traumas.

There is only so much that one human can do alone, and my Ema is the absolute superhero in my story. She saved me over and over and over again. She loved me so profoundly that her own life was flipped upside down for a long time while I struggled with my mental health.

There were times when my tornado harmed my family. So, just like an addict should be left alone when they reach a certain point of turmoil and disaster, my mother had to set boundaries with me. Lines had to be drawn. She gracefully and impossibly balanced unconditional love while standing her ground. My mother has her own book to write *(get on that, will you, Ema?)*; maybe more will be shared about our experiences together during these painful years.

There was only one place she was taking me from the hotel that night, and it definitely was not home. It was the first time I went to the hospital willingly. When I had called her, it truly was a cry for help: *Get me out of this, please.*

It was James' number I would dial when I was allowed a phone call. Though I entered the hospital willingly, once inside I forgot why. I planned an escape. I attempted to find out the workers' shifts, and I mapped out the facility so I could sneak out.

The plan was that James would come swerving in like my knight in his shining 1997 Toyota Corolla, with the door handle on the passenger side hanging off. I even convinced one of the security guards, through flirtation and persuasion, to let me use his cell phone a couple nights a week to plan the breakout. But it fell through – like such plans always did.

While I was in there, James proceeded to tattoo my name on his arm, right above where he had my face tatted. We were barely together by that time, but the mania kept us emotionally glued.

The insanity of those years is truly uncomfortable to revisit. So much was occurring simultaneously, with multiple personas and processes creating unavoidable scar tissue. I was in survival mode; when a setback or negative experience happened, I would just get up, brush off the wounds, and keep moving.

It is punishing to remember all the details of each event and then queue the events up in a traditional timeline.

If anything in the timeline is inaccurate, it is simply because only I held the keys to so many of the secrets. And I hid them proficiently – without even telling **myself** where to find them.

When I got home from the hospital's psychiatric ward, I moved back in with my family for a short time. While I was gone, they had relocated to a new home in New City, New York. It was good to be back with them.

Nothing changed with Bob after the events that transpired at the hotel, although my mother went to his office and threw a fit. She told him about my hospitalizations and other things to warn him about staying away, but she still had no idea about the extent of our relationship.

He and I carried on as usual as though nothing had ever happened.

One night while out, I saw I had missed 22 calls from James and a text that said, "If you don't call me back right now I'm going to shoot all of this up and die. Is that what you want?"

The text had a photo attached – heroin, in tiny bags all over the floor.

It was only later during the night that I finally saw the text, and James in fact had shot up all the heroin, and his heart had stopped.

But the paramedics broke his door down in time, and with the miracle of tech, science, and a little bit of God, James was revived with just a few shocks.

His family blamed me for the incident. I have not seen nor heard from him since.

To rewind just a little bit, I met G at Sal's Pizzeria. I was in the heat of my arrangement with Bob, and at the tail end of my relationship with James. I was getting comfortable with the double-triple-life thing.

When I say comfortable, I mean I was **used to it.** It had become just a regular routine for me by then.

I had started working at a young age, even though none of my jobs ever lasted past a couple of months because of my mental instability. My aberration would slither in and out on its own accord. Every time I thought I had a handle on myself, something would suddenly crash and burn in my periphery.

Anyway, by that time in my life, I had been a server, hostess and counter girl at a few different restaurants. So, with my resume, I was quickly hired at Sal's Pizzeria.

Getting a job application approved at such places was pretty swift when you wore tight T-shirts and flashed a smile as wide as your hips (along with fake references).

Even though the money from Bob was consistent, my dreams were still bigger than his monthly allowance. I had the blood of an ambitious single mother running through my veins – in my mind, the money was always for the family, for the five of us. I kept my eye on the prize and worked when I could.

I had just put the word out to some acquaintances that I needed to find my own place. Someone suggested their friend, who was looking for a third roommate. Within a couple of days, I moved in on a handshake and some loose cash.

One of the roommates was a man named Cody, and the other was a newly-sober man named Jim who sometimes had his wife and daughters visit.

Cody was a good guy. He was tan, extremely fit, shaved from his forehead down, and had a few different sex contraptions in his bedroom. Oddly, I felt safe around him.

I was freshly 18 and living with two men in their late 30's.

The comfort that I felt around older men needs to be addressed. When it started in my mid teens, I thought it was **very** cool. I would rave to my friends about dating 29-year-olds. "Boys my age are just not mature enough," I would say, ignorantly. Actually, there was some truth to that statement, in the sense that I did not relate well to boys my own age. But the deeper truth was that I was looking for validation from men who resembled my father.

A couple of years ago, when my little sister was just shy of 21, she told me she had slept with a 28-year-old man. We were in a public restaurant, and I became livid – blinded for a moment by my own traumas and projections. I began hissing at her and my eyes welled up with tears. "That's absolutely disgusting – you're a child! That man is literally a pedophile!" I spit out to her. She was confused; she had to ask me to calm down multiple times.

I believe what happened in that instance was that I had forgotten that she **was** an adult, and that their age difference did not warrant my reaction. She – at six years younger than I – always seems like she is my baby. So, I forgot for a moment – and then realized that it was actually not as awful as I initially felt that it was. It was a blackout stress response – in my mind, just for a split-second, she was me.

So when I was 18, it seemed normal to feel right at home living in a bachelor pad.

It turned out that Cody owned one of the hottest gay strip clubs in NYC. He was more straight than gay, and only put on a front for his work.

On a few different occasions, he told me that I could get work with him in the city anytime I wanted.

"You'd be a great stripper, and could make a killing – way more than at Sal's," he would say.

I would tell him that I would think about it, and always thanked him for the opportunity.

Cody dated Cami, my best friend from middle school. She was the only person who knew the truth about Bob, or about the time that I did take Cody up on a job offer – and went as a stripper to a private lesbian birthday party.

Cami worked a couple shifts at the pizzeria too; actually, she worked there before I did. One day, she started talking to me about her "very hot" manager; she said she wished that she could "get" him. And then, when she brought me in to the pizzeria for the first time, I met G – and definitely raised an eyebrow. To be truthful, I think I wanted to know if I could "get" him, since Cami could not.

G was the manager of Sal's, and had been running things there for 10 years. He and the owner, whom we called Old Man, had a close relationship.

At Sal's, G was trusted to open, close, hire, and do as he pleased.

The lonely Old Man felt a father-son bond with G, and we all knew it.

G was 28 at the time. He was short for a man, just shy of 5'6", and thick. Not fat-thick – but thick in a masculine, strong way – big quads, big arms, big hands, and a puffed, yet defined, stomach. He had a beautiful face – Italian through and through. I loved his features. His lips were big with a naturally artistic shape.

My favorite thing about G was his sense of humor, and his laugh was runner-up. That's what got me.

I had never become so devoted to getting someone to love me as I did with him, and I did not care how long I would have to wait. I went overboard with my attempts, even once showing up at his front door with a flannel and nothing underneath in the dead of winter. I just wanted to watch him want me. Offering my body was the only way I knew to really get someone's interest.

Still, he had a lot of willpower from the get-go, and stood firmly with Old Man's rule about no employee relationships.

"Too much drama," Old Man would say.

But my addictive personality rose to the occasion when it came to men who did not cave. G held it together, though, and that made me want him even more.

I was patient, but persistent.

At first he gently denied me, expressing his commitment to the restaurant's long-standing rule against romance in the workplace. I would roll my eyes, and insist that I just wanted to hang out and smoke after work.

I had asked Cami for her permission for me to pursue G, and she acted thrilled for me. "Sure! Go, girl. I mean, whatever. He's literally my boss – like it's never gonna happen anyway. Shoot your shot," she said.

I should have known better, with Cami's sly ways, that she was giving me a major test. After all, G was my boss now, too.

G and I started spending a couple nights a week making out and smoking weed at his place. We would watch movies, cuddle, and laugh.

Our connection was potent.

But within a couple of months, I saw it start eating at him. We were a complete secret. He was falling in love with me, and he was battling his values – because he was so devoted to respecting the Old Man. I knew it, but I was falling in love too, and I did not care about work rules at a local pizzeria.

Finally, one night, during one of the worst hurricanes our town had ever seen, G called me. He sounded out of breath, and had just returned from a bachelor party in New Orleans. While he was on the trip, he mentioned during a call that he'd caught a cold. So, with a spare key to his place, I snuck in and left an array of teas and herbal cold medicine on his kitchen counter.

When he got home and saw everything waiting for him in his kitchen, something hit him. So when he called, he said right away, "I'm in love with you. I'm not fighting it anymore. I've been an idiot. I want you, only you. I don't care about Sal's bullshit anymore. Will you be my girlfriend?"

I was squealing inside. I buried my face into the couch to keep from screaming out loud. *Finally!*

I had been keeping all of the details of my developing relationship with G from Cami. I had simply told her I thought he was cute and that we had hung out, but nothing more. When she asked if we had gotten physical, I lied to her – I told her we had not.

But she had a trick up her sleeve. The next day at the pizzeria, when I was off and at home, she pretended like she already knew about G and me. She went up to him and said, "Ooh, Sarah told me about your night together! I'm so happy for you guys."

G sighed very loudly, with annoyance. "Ah, so she did tell you. She told me we weren't gonna tell anyone."

Cami's eyes glazed over. Right away, G realized he had slipped up and he called to warn me.

A few hours later, Cami posted on Twitter – for the whole town to see – that I was a prostitute, and that my sugar daddy was my mom's boyfriend.

I fell back in my seat. Then I got another call from G.

"Is this true?" he asked, with a stern tone that I had not heard before.

"Of course not! I was molested, and he isn't even my mom's boyfriend," I replied.

It was the only thing I could think of saying that would save me from losing that amazing man. Besides, there was **some** truth to it. G breathed deeply, and then said, "You know what – I don't care. I'll see you later. It's OK. We're OK. Fuck Cami, she's crazy."

Of course, Cami then proceeded to let everyone at Sal's know that I was "fucking our boss."

Another employee, Mika, and her friend, Jessica, were nearly as vicious as Cami. They, too, posted all kinds of awful things on social media about me for the public to read. There were even threats to hurt me physically if they saw me – all because I was screwing our boss, and allegedly prostituting myself with my mom's theoretical boyfriend.

The picture they painted made me livid.

Countless other girls also joined in the abuse during that period, calling me names, betraying me, and threatening to physically harm me (a couple of them did). Some of them I had never hung out with; some I didn't personally know. Yet, they followed their friends' lead.

Years down the road, when I started becoming fiercely passionate about helping women love themselves, my dear mother said to me, "It's fascinating that you've devoted your life to helping other women when they've absolutely demolished you." I have pondered that comment many times, wondering where the passion materialized from, considering my many painful experiences.

Since the cat was out of the bag, and because restaurant employees love a good scandal, the news made it up to the Old Man.

One of us had to leave.

G had put too much work in to let the pizzeria go, and so I happily quit. He then asked me to move in with him, and I accepted.

The beginning of my relationship with G was on Cloud 9. We were absolutely crazy about each other. He was adoring, attentive, and affectionate. It was really the first adult relationship I had.

Though James had been even older than G, his drug addiction, his living situation (in a bedroom in his uncle's house), and his bartending job all made him less than the adult that G was. I felt like I was growing.

I promptly stepped into a housewife role as soon as I moved in. I mostly occupied myself with cleaning since I had not learned to cook yet; after cleaning, I waited for G to come home. He worked at the pizzeria from 9 a.m. to 10 p.m. most days, and would come home with his apron smelling of dough and dirt. He would walk in with his arms out, exaggerating desperation; then he'd come down the hallway, playfully whining, "Where is she? I need her!" He would then scoop me up and carry me back down the hallway while kissing my neck, breathing me in and holding me tight. I would giggle, squirm out, and tell him to go wash that damn dough off and then meet me in bed.

It was the same thing every night for a while. I absolutely loved it. I remember the way we would fold into and wrap around each other, and the way he would wake me up with the sweetest touch. I would open my eyes, and he would be staring at me – lovingly. His gaze would turn into a gentle grin when he noticed I was rising. "There is nothing in this world as beautiful as you," he would say, with his eyes locked on mine.

I would close them again, keeping the smile on my face, basking in the nectar of adoration. There was a physical closeness with him that felt like love to me.

Though G treated me like a queen, and we loved each other in many ways, my instability was still alive and well.

Bob was still in the picture – lurking – and I was becoming a notorious runner.

"Wherever you go, there you are, Mima," my mom would always say. That drove me up the wall.

Deep in my soul, I felt that moving to a place other than New York, where I seemed to stay broken into a million pieces, was the answer. My mother could not tell me differently.

The first time I left was to Oahu, Hawaii.

G and I were living together, and I had signed up for a community college in New York (one of my attempts at being "normal" in between my random jobs).

I earned my GED, filled out all the paperwork to receive financial aid, and soon found myself sitting in a photography classroom. Everyone was really proud of me. My mom even came over on the first morning of my classes to take pictures. I think, for a moment, she thought the insanity was over.

I was not even through my first week of classes when I received a text from my friend Sheri.

"Wanna move to Hawaii for free with me?"

I smirked and responded, "Say less."

I left in the middle of my classes. It was clear – that college stuff was not for me. Anticipating my big move, my whole body shook with excitement – and that old manic feeling rose up in my blood.

I tossed my books into the trash can, flung open the building doors, raced to my Jeep Wrangler, and hopped in with a high that I was unable to control.

No one could stop me. My mother sighed and knew there was nothing she could do.

Surprisingly, G fully supported my move to Hawaii. He said that he loved me no matter what, and that he knew that I needed to do it. He wrote me a six-page goodbye letter, making me promise that I would not read it until I was on the plane.

I cried as I read his loving words and took off from JFK to Honolulu.

I had a job waiting for me in an operation run by a couple of Israeli business owners, although now I am sure they were finessing the entire thing. They paid for the flight, and I moved into a three-bedroom apartment in Waikiki with three other girls. We were to stand at a booth in the mall, selling hair straighteners. Our pitch was that those particular straighteners actually would heal the hair, rather than burn it the way most styling tools do.

We had to stop strangers, using our charm, and get them to sit in our chair. Then, hopefully, we would sell them a straightener and earn a commission. We did not get paid otherwise.

But the four of us had a shared car, an apartment, and lived by the beach. I also had a stash of cash from Bob. I did not give a shit about my job or making commissions, and you could not pay me enough for me to become a pushy salesperson.

I never made a single dollar. Within about two months, I was sobbing on the phone with G, begging him to let me come home.

He took me back; he always did.

I ran three more times over the next few years. I moved back to Israel, then to St. Thomas, then to California. And I always made a grand, declarative announcement that I was "really going for good this time."

In the course of all of my runs, G always dropped me off and picked me up from the airport. He always carried me home, took care of me through my dark depressions and manic episodes, and loved me through it all.

trained to trigger people – stayed quiet for a few moments before dropping a bomb on me in front of everyone.

"So, you're a prostitute. Say it how it is."

I knew well that I had dressed up the story to sound more like I was an innocent child when it started, violently forced against my will, and trapped with no way out. I took no accountability for my part in all of it.

The coach saw right through me, and it was the best thing that ever happened to me. That type of truth-telling was the all-powerful beginning.

My eyes welled up with tears. I sat down, implying that I was extremely offended and done with the exercise.

"Uh-uh, GET UP," he demanded.

I felt myself becoming 5 years old at that moment. Still crying, I crossed my arms, put my head down, and shook it back and forth.

No, no, no.

I did eventually get up and faced the conversation head-on. We cleared up the truth of the matter: that me, having been 16, and him, then in his 40's,

I did not go back to that workshop for years. But I eventually completed the courses, although that was one of the most challenging things I would ever do – and I almost quit, again, multiple times.

After I went back to the workshop, Mom was usually somewhere close by, making sure I stayed.

As I looked at the "hard stuff" more and more, I even took level 2 and 3 workshops – Advanced, and Leadership. I was still living my double life throughout those times, which brings an interesting question to the table.

Is it possible that the **work is working** even if one continues on with the self-sabotage? Are the breakthroughs and tools sticking to us somewhere deep inside, collecting dust but retaining their value, until we are ready to reach for them and use them? I was genuinely passionate about self-discovery, health, and personal growth at the end of my teens. But no matter what I did, I could not let go of the abusive men, the lies, and my desire for validation.

The part of me that read the books, took the courses, and tried different modalities of health and automatically made the situation molestation and statetory rape – regardless of the details, regardless of whether I had said "no," or not.

Today, I am aware that I was mentally unstable, and that I was not to blame. I do not hate myself anymore for what I did; but I chose to take full responsibility that day. I picked my head up and lifted my chest.

I am not a victim.

Regardless of the personal growth and the eye-openers that were revealed in the workshops, I was still wearing the veils. I was still unsteadily holding my guises together with a shriveled string.

All of my growth experiences were tiny seeds, so miniscule that it would be years before I truly saw any yield from the soil.

Much like the rise of bamboo, which takes seven years to surface and then one day shoots up and out like an arrow from a bow, my exodus from my delusional life was unhurried.

I was finally ready to move on with my life and get out of New York permanently. This thing that I was looking for was not there; I knew it for sure. To me, it felt like an absolutely dead town. After everything that had happened there in my life, there was utterly nothing left for me in New York.

One random morning, G was dropping me off at the gym. With one leg out of the car, I turned and looked at him. I started talking. Everything spilled out about how unbearably painful it was for me to stay in New York.

I could not do it anymore. I could **smell** everything that had happened to me there. It was in every corner store, in every bar, at the mall, and on every street. I knew that everyone looked at me and saw **"slut"** written on my forehead.

G was always supportive of me following my heart, even if it meant breaking his. And as I looked into his eyes, I saw how little he had left for a fight.

It had been four long years of exhausting and gnawing love. There was a lot of love – but also a lot of fights, abandonment, and irreversible hurt. I noticed that his under-eyes were darker and more tired than I had ever seen them. I knew I had taken a toll on his emotional viability; it would take a long time for him to move on from the damage I had done.

"Okay, baby. I understand. I love you. Go fly."

I got out of the car and felt a liberation course through me.

It was the same effervescent and activating liberation I felt every time I walked away from any man.

After the downward spiral of being with Noah, I never wanted anyone to the extent of excluding anyone else. I never truly wanted to keep anyone.

Whenever a breakup happened in my adulthood, I felt exhilarated. As I became more passionate about making changes within myself, I came to feel that it was impossible to make changes and continue to grow when a man was in the picture.

They seemed to only keep me trapped in my old ways. When I was with a man, I would get lazy.

I would sleep in, eat out, drink, smoke, do things I did not want to do, and give him too much of me – with too little left to give to myself.

So when a relationship was over, I always said a silent *thank you* for freedom to whatever god was out there.

I used to think that my ache to be alone meant I was not supposed to ever be in a relationship, and I just needed to kick that addiction.

Now I know – it was not about that. I was only attracting what my inner world was stirring up – worthlessness, lack of commitment, messy relationships, pain, addictions, dishonesty, manipulation, and more. Those "virtues" showed up in the form of men. And I lived with them for the majority of my life, because misery **loves** company.

So after I thanked God and had a few moments of peace, I would fall asleep and forget – again.

I could not leave New York without my mother and little sister. My brother was still running and crashing on repeat, and he had no interest in leaving.

I put money from Bob aside to get me, my mom, and my little sister out. Esther had been long gone for years – she moved back to Israel in her teens and still lives there to this day.

My mother's seasonal depression was at its worst during that year, and I vowed to take her somewhere warm and away from the traumas that New York inflicted on us. We all have equally difficult biographies.

We packed up my Jeep to the brim, and the three of us took off – for good.

There is not one among us who was not forced to sacrifice her essence at the altar of survival to submit to values that were not her own.

- Jalaja Bonheim

Wherever you go, there you are was the major theme at this point in my life. Every time I attempted different ways to escape myself, my mother repeated that saying to me, over and over. I started to realize that she was right. I would find out that I could not outrun, finesse, or tune out the truth with a relocation. The truth follows you like a tail or shadow.

Things only got worse for me when we landed in Naples, Florida. However, they got better for my family, and that mattered to me most of all.

We chose Naples because it was far away from New York, yet an easy drive with the few belongings we had; and it was near the beach. My mother also had a friend there who helped us look for a place before our arrival.

The money I saved from Bob covered our expenses for about a year.

My mother was finally able to step out of poverty when she began creating her own community and developing her career. She met a good man, too; I was proud of her. And my sister was happy and making friends at her new school.

Above all, we were finally living together, by the beach.

At least I had the beach.

I started working at a gym in town and made some friends, including my boss, and his girlfriend, who was my co-worker.

They were sexually dominant and had a fetish for finding young girls and making them their third musketeer in the bedroom. I fell into that situation for a short time, while getting belligerently drunk at the bars and clubs we would visit together.

From there, over the next six months, I went on to be the plaything to a couple of other abominable people in town. I drank to a dangerous extent and was blacking out regularly. I experienced a handful of horrifying incidents that I could hardly recall afterward. Even if I could remember it all, I would prefer to forget.

I lost friends, was exploited and violated, and somehow none of it registered with me until much later. I lied to people, but truths surfaced, making me a laughingstock. A video went around town of me having a threesome.

This specific portion of my story is especially agonizing to recall and tell. I get ferocious chills up my spine as I type. Shame relentlessly tries to creep in. I take a deep breath and remind myself that I am safe, and that I'm no longer her – and even so, she is loved.

I felt extremely compelled to find another form of income other than Bob. I craved freedom from his financial support, and I searched tirelessly for jobs where I would not have a boss who could fire me for instability or inconsistency.

Money and men were blurred into one thing with me. It was the only combination that I knew was a sure thing. I could **always** get money through men. Men had been throwing money at me for my time and my body for years.

During the crucial years in my youth when my brain was still developing, and where most young girls were getting allowances or planning for college, I was learning how to use my appearance to make quick cash. For a long time, that was the only way I ever would earn fast money.

I had no understanding of savings, investments, or taxes. That lack of knowledge proved to be detrimental as I came into adulthood. It kept me farther and farther away from true abundance. Many times, I would look up and ask the sky – even years into running my own company – Why am I still struggling? Why am I still selling pictures of my body online for extra income? What am I doing wrong?

I learned to trust that I could generate income with nothing but my own heart and passion. I needed to cut off any type of sexual exchange – cold turkey – if I was ever going to create a clean, abundant, and honest relationship with money.

But there was no clear pathway for me – everything was distorted and dishonest. True abundance cannot live in that kind of place.

I understand the conversation that I had with the universe a little bit better now, and I know that I was clearly expressing that I trusted men to provide financial freedom. Men were my comfort zone. I (eventually) realized that nothing could possibly grow there.

I had promised my mother I would stay for a year to help her get on her feet, but time was moving quickly. I couldn't live with my family in Naples for much longer.

My relationship with the mirror was a painful one. The savage ways of horny men eased that pain, offering me a debauched way out of loving myself. The men did it for me, temporarily, one after the other, with no space in between to breathe my own air.

Though I did not need to do the next job I would take, my experience with men thus far had created a distorted reality for me. It seemed that the only thing I was really good at was giving my body over for men's pleasure. I felt lifeless, with no natural gifts or callings.

And so, I was recruited. And honestly, the pitch was enticing. A mutual friend connected me with Annika, a ruthless, bleached-blonde Russian girl in her early 20s. Annika lived in an extravagant, top-floor penthouse with an expansive view of the city. The windows stretched from floor to ceiling, and the dining room table matched their length. Her closet was filled with designer shoes and purses. She had rock-solid breast implants, silicone injections in each butt cheek, and a chihuahua with a pink collar. She and the dog went everywhere together in her jet-black Mercedes Benz.

At the time, I did not know that there were different ways to live in abundance. I thought that Annika's lifestyle was what prosperity looked like; clearly, she was doing well. Coming from a life where **anything** extra was rare, and having a scarcity mindset that was running wild, seeing a girl like that was intoxicating.

For a little while, I followed her lead. I began to furtively fly into New York from Florida for a week at a time to make some money. I would also see Bob if I had to, and then I would duck back home to my mom's when the job was done. I would always just say that I was visiting friends from back home in New York.

Opulent was the name of an underground erotic massage parlor located on the upper east side of New York City. After a few conversations with Annika about the way it worked, and after I dissected the level of their discretion, I decided to apply. The business, run by a woman named Claudia, had a seamless operation. The entrance was a simple white door on a corner of Third Avenue. Once a customer was buzzed in, a security guard would check them in and lead them down a staircase to a lower-level entrance.

Upon entering the parlor, there would be no sign of anything dubious or peculiar. Every step taken in the establishment reinforced *Opulent's* facade of a high-end spa.

The decor was tasteful and luxurious, with lighting that instantly calmed the nerves. Soothing and sensual music played at the perfect volume from hidden speakers. There was no way to tell if the music was coming from within the walls, or from the extravagant plant and flower arrangements. The entrance hall even had an elegant fountain.

The sophisticated front desk attendant had a chic bluetooth headset, and she wore a two-piece skirt suit (you know, that suit that all the girls wear when they are playing a professional role in the movies – with the high-waisted skirt and button-down shirt that makes you look at your leggings and crop top and think, *How does she do it?*).

We all wore uniforms that looked like old-school nurse costumes with a sailor-suit twist. I have no fucking idea why. If I had been running the place, we would have all been in Agent Provocateur mode, with silk kimonos that stopped right at the upper thigh.

My name at *Opulent* was Jodie for a while; when I entered that space, I left my birth name and story behind. There, I was something and someone completely different. The takeaway was up to $2K a day (for a girl who gets good tips, anyway) and I got pretty good at it.

All the men who entered the establishment were different, with different stories and schedules. I would talk to some of them – if they were interested in talking. Some of them genuinely were – and I would share my dreams of writing a book, or of being an actress or singer, as I massaged their naked bodies before whispering the magic words, "You can turn over whenever you're ready." Even if the clock said that there was still 3o minutes left, I would usually purr those words in their ears, with the hope of getting them out early. It was a trick we all knew well.

It was a work-whenever-you'd-like type of environment. And I had some regulars for the short time I was there.

Throughout that period, my delusion was raging. I had convinced myself that I was the furthest thing from a sex worker. If I had been twirling on a pole, or on the corner of a street, then I most definitely would have been one – but no one knew what I was doing, so therefore I was not.

Plus, the "quality" of that specific spa enabled my delusion, convincing me that it was some really elite stuff. Somewhere, because of some movie or story, I must have learned and believed that the only real sex work was done by a trashy prostitute standing on a corner in Vegas.

Well, shit. Come to find out I had covered about half a dozen jobs in the sex-work industry. But at least I could tell myself that I never stood on a corner in Las Vegas. That kept me hopeful.

When my shift was over at *Opulent*, I walked back up those dark stairs, past the security guard and pushed open the heavy, opaque side door that opened onto the bustling city. The sunlight on Third Avenue would blind me for a moment, washing the day's deeds away, and I would proceed to strut down the street and only look forward.

Soon, though, I became too sick about it to stay any longer.

Back in Naples, I got ready to move out of my mom's place. I had driven to Miami a few times and decided to move there. In no time, I had platinum blonde hair with extensions, enormous fake breasts, a Brazilian butt lift, acrylic nails, and a studio apartment 10 minutes from the strip. Miami photographers took a liking to me, and I was the perfect candidate to splash all over social media. My following on Instagram grew rapidly.

I am questioned on two topics, a lot: how I grew my social media presence, and if my body is natural. Throwing on bikinis and heels, accentuating beauty by any means necessary, and hiring makeup artists specifically to build appeal to Instagram followers was how I did it. I stepped into another persona with ease. I was a natural at being artificial.

The thing is, though, I never needed to do any of it. I did not even really want to. My mind was under the spell I had cast – the one telling me to please **them** at all costs. My true self did not have control; I was not even aware of what was truly happening at that point. My mission to please and also free myself from Bob overpowered everything.

I searched for ways to contort myself, but my body was already naturally shaped like an hourglass. My sisters and mother are the genetic confirmation of that, and they have never had any work done. It was all there already, undoubtedly.

Still, I was so delusional and at such a dangerous level of body dysmorphia that I actually did things to my body that were completely redundant. I went under the knife to change something that was already perfect.

As a result, I had many health issues arise after my breast augmentation and Brazilian butt lift – acne, digestive issues, brain fog, pain, and physical numbness. Nevertheless, the dysmorphia and addiction to enhancing my appearance only grew.

Although my appearance was based on deception, I did find an adoring audience for my body after the surgeries. I knew I was attractive to everyone else. I walked around proud, exuding sex, seemingly confident. My followers on social media were growing, companies were sending me free clothes, and celebrities regularly fawned over me. I was playing a twisted game, descending deeper into a spiritual hole, again.

Miami was a dark place for me. I met a social media manager, Ken, who promised me the world. Ken was known for grabbing all the sexiest girls in Miami and growing their Instagram followings through a convoluted process of hashtags and connections. He would send us off to photo shoots every other day and promised that eventually he would get us paid gigs. The photo shoots were usually raunchy (though back then they seemed pretty high-quality to me, since the pictures were smooth and professional-looking). But now, looking back at most of the pictures, I realize it was nothing but selling sex – ass, ass, ass.

While I was pursuing my mission to be seen in any way, shape, or form, I took a job as a shot girl at an enormous strip club in downtown Miami. It was known as **the** strip club – the one that the rappers mentioned in their songs. It was the one where all the celebrities spent tens of thousands a night

Miami, 2017: Who is she? I sometimes really felt like I did not know her. But I loved her so much. She wanted to be loved; she wanted to be free. She did not know there was a universe inside of her, much larger than her ass, that had infinite capabilities.

on different dancers, throwing $100 bills in the air while bottle after bottle was brought to their tables.

I worked there for a couple of months, my shift starting around 9 or 10 p.m. and ending around 4 or 5 a.m. I was really good at that job. Too good, some said. The dancers whispered and gave me nasty glares when the night was slow, their pockets still dry, while men were buying my entire tray of shots just to sit and talk with me.

I was just good at flirting, and I did it with a sparkle in my eye that was ostensibly genuine. Along with the flirtation came a studied Julia-Roberts-like laugh that always got them hooked, and I kept my legs crossed like a good girl.

I liked it for a few nights, but soon the hours took a toll on my body. I kept up my cocaine habit and would sleep the day away after I walked into my apartment at sunrise.

I got **so close** to stepping on stage. I was raking in almost $1000 a night just selling Jell-O shots while wearing fishnets and a skimpy bodysuit. When the whispers in my ear grew louder about my cash-making potential – if I would just step **one** level off the ground and wrap my hands around that pole, I almost caved.

But I could not bring myself to do it. To me, for some reason, becoming a stripper would mean **no going back – ever.**

After six months in Miami, I cut my lease short and ran. Another city that swallows people whole was calling.

Hollywood is a place where they'll pay you a thousand dollars for a kiss and fifty cents for your soul. I know, because I turned down the first offer often enough and held out for the fifty cents.
- Marilyn Monroe

There was no darker world that I ever visited than the world of Hollywood. There was nowhere more empty, more confusing, and more stripping of my self-love.

I came to believe that there was not a single woman there, including myself, who was true. And likewise, there was not a single man there who was not over-compensating or selling himself. All the faces wore makeup, all the bodies dressed in costumes. All conversations were practiced scripts, borrowed realities, and old stories.

All of us were seeking validation in some way. Some of us were seeking God, some were seeking love and power, some were seeking a handout or connection. Some just needed an ear to listen to them. Many simply wanted confirmation that they, too, deserved the wealth, fame, and success that the current "man of the hour" enjoyed.

Celebrity. We all wanted it – wanted to be around it – and we all would pretend to be nonchalant about it, like it was not obvious. And the ones who had it were mindlessly swimming in the praise, fame, and continuous validation. All in pain, all wasting money, all hiding in plain sight. Having some of the world's most recognizable faces pursue me would lead me into some of the most fascinating and challenging experiences of my life.

Remember that "grandiose" life that I said I felt connected to at a young age? The rooms of Hollywood felt like the closest thing to that. My mind was still unclear about exactly what I was looking for, but all I knew was that it was **enormous** there. Those years were wild and impactful. They were also humiliating and nerve-wracking.

After being invited behind the scenes a few times, I realized I had a knack for befriending and attracting some of the most famous people in the world.

But I always knew I did not belong. I never had an interest in their specific lifestyles. I wanted financial freedom like they had – like we all do – yet, the ways they spent their money and time enraged me.

Mirror.

Even so, by that time in my life, I was used to doing things that made me sick. I drowned in it sometimes, still in my pattern of punishing myself, finding myself in places that my body was screaming to leave.

In the end, I stuck around for probably what was too long, dated a handful of them, and racked up lots of luxurious life experiences. I indulged in the hope that the abundance would rub off on me and save me. Or maybe it would pick me, like a flower.

I took first-class flights, ate meals prepared by private chefs, and sat beside them in elite London casinos while they would gamble an amount that most of us would not dream of seeing in a lifetime.

I rode in the black cars, garnered security guard protection, boated on yachts, and flew in private jets. I accepted the gifts, and, of course, I kept all the secrets they always shared.

Most of my encounters started on Instagram.

The exploitation of young girls by powerful men is happening every day, in many different ways. It is a much more pervasive problem in this country than most people realize. Even though we have now all heard of Jeffrey Epstein, I do not think that most people relate emotionally to what he did, and the kind of harm that he perpetuated.

To my knowledge, this is not yet widely discussed, but social media is the new high-end escort system. It is a glamorized, hidden-in-plain-sight, prostitutes' playground. It is 2023 now, and celebrities or men with money to spend can contact anyone they desire, and vice versa.

Put together a rapper with a blue check (or a nobody who sends some quick cash) and a small-town hottie, and what you get is a few messages exchanged before a flight is booked and a one-night stand takes place. Sometimes it takes just a couple hours and she is on a flight back home.

Maybe she never hears from him again – or maybe he starts paying some bills and taking her on some lavish trips. All she has to do is give her body. All she has to do is say **yes.**

Some of the most renowned A-list celebrities – names that you would have to live under a rock to have never heard of – are messaging young girls for a quick flight and fuck while their wife and kids are at home. You would be shocked.

You might say that "escort" or "prostitute" are harsh words to use when that is not the girl's initial intention. But something always feels wrong about it within her spirit after the empty encounter. Unfortunately, that **is** what is happening.

There were two particular high-rollers who would have a lasting effect on me. One was a world-famous athlete, and the other was an artist who is quite arguably the most recognized person on the planet. One I was involved with for five years, while I spent only five days with the other. And interestingly enough, the experiences were interconnected.

Brian was a true NBA superstar. I had come across a photo of him a few weeks prior to our meeting, and I fell in love with his features. I stared at the picture for a long time, like an artist admiring a sculpture – in complete awe. I told myself I would find him, and that he would be mine *(a reminder to be careful what you wish for, and that our minds can truly create things out of thin air)*.

One night, my girlfriend Cheri and I popped into a famed nightclub in the heart of the city. After about an hour, I was bored and overwhelmed with how loud it was. I grabbed Cheri's hand to leave. The room was packed, and moving about was a challenge – but all of a sudden, a rope was lifted. With a little nudge from a security guard, we were in the VIP section at a spacious table.

When I looked up, he – Brian – was standing on the couch looking down at me. I wore a sheer white dress with a white bodysuit underneath. We spent the night eyeing each other.

"You're coming with us to the afterparty," he said into my ear with the music still blasting. It was well past 4 a.m. The mania butterflies were **flying.**

Once in the suite, drinks were passed around, while girls, other athletes, rappers, and wannabes swarmed the place.

"Can you get me a drink, please?" I asked, with an innocent smile on my face. Brian took a while to get it for me, because he was stopped by every person in the room who wanted to have a moment with the star. But he eventually made it over.

"Sorry, that took me a minute," he said.

Then he spilled the drink on me accidentally, and I took it as an opportunity to laugh, flirt, and get his attention on me.

"You better get something to clean this off my pristine white dress!" I exclaimed.

We giggled as he did his best to wipe the stain off the white fabric.

Shortly after 6 a.m., a hotel attendant knocked on the door and entered with a buffet for the party.

An array of bacon, eggs, sausages, waffles, juices, coffee, pastries, fruit and more spread across the extended cart. Everyone took a plate, and I watched as Brian took his out on the balcony. The sun was rising, and I followed him out.

We talked a bit – mostly, I asked him questions, but I also talked about myself. He was a talker too, but he never really said much. I told him I didn't realize he was so famous, and he said he liked that.

I found him absolutely enthralling. I think it was partly my fascination with the fact that I had powerfully manifested that moment.

"You look like a good kisser," I responded, lamely.

"Oh yeah?" he said in a low tone with an eyebrow raised.

I went for it – and he was not a good kisser at all. But I did not care. We kissed and stumbled into the bathroom, which was the size of my apartment. Suddenly we were completely alone, and the party outside was forgotten.

We had strong physical chemistry, and by that point I knew very well how to create intimacy and a show for a stranger.

Brian walked up slowly while I fixed my hair in the mirror; he held me from behind with slow swaying movements. Still clothed, we admired each other's reflections.

He took my dress off slowly and kept his eyes on the outspread mirror in front of us.

"This all you?" he asked, painting the air with his hands, following the shape of my body.

"All me," I said.

I kept my heels on, and we fucked for two hours, with two award-winning fake orgasms on my end.

When we walked out of the bathroom, we looked around to find that only a few people were left. Cheri was one of them, and she was not happy with me. I put my number in Brian's phone and we said our goodbyes.

Halfway down the hall, I stopped and realized that I had accidentally given him an old number. I ran back to the room and knocked, hoping I wasn't too late. He and his friends all stood by the door as I typed in the correct number and then took off.

I wonder sometimes – if I had not realized that it was the wrong number, would the next five years of my life have looked dramatically different?

I was infatuated. And I was delusional. I was convinced that Brian and I had something special – and every day, I tried to prove I was a woman worthy of someone of his stature. Even if months passed where I didn't see him, I would spend that time becoming what he wanted – someone more sexy, more successful, more desirable.

The reality, as I know it now, was that I willingly responded every time he beckoned me. I sought his validation even though I never truly felt a connection. He was a mess, in a lot of ways – a raging alcoholic, a hardcore partier, and an avid drug user. I frequently found myself running to him when I got a call that he "needed" me. I was always put on a first-class flight or private jet; and

I always felt like I was drawing closer to my own abundance when I mooched off of his.

Sometimes he would be too drunk to even do anything intimate, and he would pass out in my lap after venting about the hardships of fame. He mumbled often, and I recall many conversations where I could not understand a word he said. He was usually on something.

Brian eventually invited me into his home with his family, and he had me around during some of his lowest points. That made me feel really special.

Still, I was never his girlfriend – and no one outside of our immediate circle knew of our entanglement. He kept me hanging on – he told me that if he became ready for a relationship, it would be me. He would frequently give me a speech about how much I meant to him – and how I was one of the only people for whom he would do **anything.**

So, I believed him, and waited around for years – used and lied to, over and over. And I knew it was a lie, every time.

After all, we were mirroring each other.

We ended up taking a long break shortly after an incident at one of his homes in California.

I had come over to his place with bags of groceries and I planned to cook dinner. There had been some discussion and a couple of rain checks before we actually solidified the plans. For some reason, I was excited to prove myself in the kitchen.

Sometimes I really did not understand why he even wanted me around. Often, he would busy himself elsewhere on the property, working on other things for hours. While he was occupied, I would read – or talk to his maid, or trainers, or his mother.

Nonetheless, I was there on that particular evening whipping up sweet potatoes, mac 'n' cheese, and chicken.

Cooking is a happy place for me. My mother was a caterer for some time. She also had a gift for creating delicious meals out of thin air. There may have only been three ingredients left in our kitchen, and while no one was able to think of a dish to whip up, Ema always figured it out.

As for me, I did not start cooking until my early 20s. I was beginning to understand healthy eating in a new way, so I was just grateful to find my way around the kitchen. A lot of what I did simply came from memories of watching my mother; I would find my hands crushing garlic or peeling a vegetable before realizing I had never done it before. My body just knew what to do.

So here I was in Brian's kitchen, and even though I was vibing to some good music and dancing around the counters and stoves as I mixed and chopped, I felt the hurt creeping up in my chest. Brian was ignoring my presence the entire time and hanging out in the back living room, which was a five-minute walk to the kitchen. Worlds apart.

I was disappointed and felt self-conscious. I had imagined him sitting on the counter and playfully spending time with me while I cooked. What I **imagined** and what actually **was** were never the same when it came to Brian.

One of his friends, who I had never met, came into the kitchen; he stopped when he saw me putting the sweet potatoes in the oven. He asked, "Hey, are you the new cook or maid?"

The question absolutely outraged me – and woke me up at the same time.

Fuck this guy, I thought to myself. *He is so self-absorbed back there that his friends think I'm the help.*

I felt a tidal wave of shame and humiliation. *I look like a fucking idiot,* I thought. Other intrusive thoughts filled my mind. It was the last straw; I had experienced so many similar moments with him already, where the degradation had been obvious.

I took the sweet potatoes out of the oven early, made him a big plate of food, and then walked to the back room. In front of his friends, I handed him the plate, kissed him on the cheek, and left. I did not care if the potatoes were still hard. I imagined him taking a bite and laughing with everyone about the poor cooking.

I felt foolish. *He didn't even offer to pay for the groceries when I cooked a buffet meal for him, his trainers, his dad and his other stupid fuckin' friends.*

I drove away sobbing. My negative loop was on full blast. I felt like I could throw up from embarrassment and I went into a spiral of dark thoughts. I could not stop thinking about how long I had been throwing myself at this man, replaying every event where he disrespected me and where I disrespected myself.

I thought about all the years of hoping and praying to God that something I did would finally make him turn around and say, "Wow, this is the one. She's like nobody else, and I don't want anyone else." And then he would give up the bullshit, the clubbing, the strippers, the alcohol, the self-inflicted abuse, and the obsession with fame and designer clothes. And then he would just go to his games and work, and cuddle and play in nature with me and do art and …

I am out of my fucking mind.

We did not talk for months.

do not look for healing
at the feet of those
who broke you
- Rupi Kaur, Milk and Honey

I started seeing someone else.

Jerry and I were not officially dating, but I was smitten – and in a moment of weakness, I thought I might have found love in the midst of my chaos.

Jerry was a wolf in sheep's clothing. He used me for money, sex, and free rides. He was not a celebrity – he was mooching off of some of them, too. He was another reflection in my world of mirrors.

There was some love there – if I can call it that. We had a short period of time when we actually connected and enjoyed each other. I even felt a brief moment of emotional support from him. But soon, we were toxically attached – on and off, unable to let go. The rage built on both ends – he learned about my dishonesty, and I learned about his narcissism and manipulative styles. He too had many secrets; he was just better at keeping them than I was.

We were addicted to the mess of it all.

A couple months into our dance, I flew out to see one of my girlfriends whose father was in the hospital. I used her father's illness as my reason for traveling so suddenly.

However, while at my friend's place on the East Coast, Brian texted me to check in.

He did that often over the years, and it always messed with me. I would get excited, thinking that I was going to see him, but he would just say something like, "Wassup, just checking on you." I would roll my eyes and fall back into my seat. I used to think that his communication might mean he genuinely cared about me, if he was not just reaching out for sex. But I now think he was just making sure that he still had access to me.

"Where ya at?" he asked. I raised an eyebrow and realized that he did not know I was in his area. My heart started racing. Although I very often put on a front about him, and even said that I had strategically paused our relationship, I still wanted so badly for him to fully choose me – express his desire, beg for me to come to him – anything. He also had a knack for pretending like nothing had happened, like it had not been months since we had seen each other. I always played along, never wanting to seem too dramatic or emotional.

"I'm on the East Coast just hangin' with a girlfriend. What's up?" I responded.

"You're in my hood and you didn't even let me know?!" he exclaimed.

Got 'em.

I felt a satisfied smile creep up on my face. He asked me to come over. At first I told him that I couldn't; that I was only there for my friend.

"Come on. One night. I'll send you a car. My chef is around; she'll cook us some dinner. I haven't seen you in a minute. Let's just vibe."

Ugh. Fine.

I caved.

I gathered myself to head over to his place, about 45 minutes away. When I arrived, his assistant and his father were there. We all goofed around in the kitchen while Brian and I danced around the space, poking fun at each other and teasing. Since the beginning, we had a sarcastic and playful dynamic, never going too deep.

His chef whipped up some food, and afterward we just hung out in the living room, the two of us aimlessly scrolling on our phones while his on-call chiropractor worked on his body.

I always felt an empty spiritual space in all of his enormous homes.

Often while I was with him, I would experience a recurring uncertainty of what to do with myself. He would play video games, have some sort of in-home service like a tattoo appointment or trainer, or pick outfits for a trip with his assistant. I would stand there, trying to look comfortable. My spirit felt so out of place. And every time, I would hear a whisper in my ear saying something like, *What are you even doing here?*

I thought back to the day that I had come over to cook for him and felt so asininely disrespected that I stormed off and did not speak to him for months.

Was I in the right? Was he just being himself? Had I expected more from someone who never gave me anything but less than the bare minimum? Was it an overreaction on my part? Or was it not even the situation – but simply my spirit, again, begging for me to wake up?

I never had any true fun with Brian. Although his lavish life offered anything he desired, and I could have asked for anything, there was a blandness in the air around him that I could not put my finger on. We were very different people, from different walks of life, and with different hobbies. I did not understand his career, nor did I want to. Sports were of no interest to me, and shopping for brand names didn't tickle my fancy.

As I look back on him now, it is almost like he was made up solely of sports and designer clothes. I never knew how to truly connect with this man, other than through sex. I am still certain that there was depth to him, and I saw sparks of it in a moment of humor, or a short intimate conversation.

At times, I felt a deep desire to dive into his inner self and recover everything that the industry had taken from his soul; but I lost so much of myself thinking I was equipped to do so.

That night, after dinner and all of his required engagements, we went upstairs to take a bath and wind down. After a few minutes, he started to open up. I watched him sink deeper into relaxation as the flavor in the air lowered his guard. I rubbed his neck and listened as he shared his desires for the future, and I heard every detail of his crippling self-doubt. I felt him in a more profound way at that moment.

Something about the setting and his opening up brought us to make love without protection that night.

"You better not ever give this to anyone else," he said as he wrapped his hand gently around my neck and peered deeply into my eyes.

A month later, I found out I was pregnant.

Both my spirituality and my sexuality
were very powerful, but each was
in a compartment of its own,
and they did not touch.
- Jalaja Bonheim, from Aphrodite's Daughters

I was back home in Los Angeles when I found out. I sat with it for a couple of days, flabbergasted by the news. When I finally texted Brian about it, he immediately asked for my bank information so that he could pay for the abortion.

When I saw that he had sent me $10,000, I texted him.

"Uh, Sir, abortions don't cost that much," I noted.

"I just wanna make sure you're good," he replied.

I knew he wanted to make sure I took care of it, with a little incentive.

When I went to my doctor's appointment, I found out there was a possible complication with the pregnancy. Also, I would need to wait a week or so to have the procedure, so it could be seen clearly on the ultrasound. But there was interference in the timetable. I had plans to visit my family in Israel for two weeks, with a stop in Dubai to meet a man who had sent me $10,000 in response to a few messages that were exchanged between us on Instagram. I felt obligated, so the abortion would have to wait until I returned.

During that time, I shared my situation with my closest girlfriends.

They egged me on: "If you kept this baby, you could relax. You'd be taken care of financially for the rest of your life. You know who this man is; he's loaded." It was a challenging time for me, as I pondered on what I really wanted, and who I really was.

My thoughts circled back to my truth, my purpose – that fire burning in the chest of that little girl. You know, the one who thought she was meant for something bigger?

Was this what "bigger" looked like? It was hard to see it that way. I understood why some women might want to have a baby by a famous athlete, and be well taken care of. But to me, it looked like a prison with no escape – something that might actually keep me locked in the hell that I'd been living in for a long time.

I never intended to stay in it forever.

I was still living dangerous double and triple lives; but my divine guidance kept speaking to me – in fact, it was powerfully present as I considered my situation.

I was sick during my entire journey to Dubai and Israel. I was puking in the stalls, puking when the plane took off, and puking throughout my time in the two different countries. Thankfully, Dubai Guy had booked me my own hotel suite and wasn't pushy about spending a ton of time together. The couple of nights we went out to dinner were difficult, as I did my best to hide how I was really feeling. I kept up my bruised guise of a "good girl." I even improvised a story to avoid sleeping with him; I told him I hadn't slept with anyone in over a year and I wanted to get to know him better. My belly gurgled as I spoke the enormous lie with an innocent smile.

When Jerry came to pick me up after my return flight, he found me lying in a fetal position on the floor by the LAX baggage claim. I had told him the truth, albeit with little white lies intertwined.

I had my doctor's appointment set for the following day. Jerry came along.

I found out that I was cleared to have the procedure, and that I could have it that same day. They gave me a Valium and waited about 15 minutes for it to take hold.

I laid back in a dentist-like chair, and I felt **everything.** I felt the tools, the cold clamps, the metal, the pain, **everything**. I cried the whole time – not only from the physical pain, but also from the unalloyed disgrace. Jerry held my hand the whole time, even though he knew I was pregnant with another man's baby.

After that surgery, my body changed. My emotions almost completely shut down. I went into a **deeper** spiritual descent, and continued to throw my body away.

I used to feel that I had **some** respect in my relationships with Jerry and Brian, but soon there seemed to be none. It was almost as if they **felt** me lose all respect for myself – and along with mine, went theirs.

Bob was still around occasionally. He was frequently coming to LA for work.

The way I was used up was degrading.

The way I was treated was dispiriting.

The way I convinced myself I was a victim was mystifying. Staying with men who were so toxic to my joy was self-defilement, yet I begged for their validation every day.

I kept the relationships separate, although Jerry knew the truth. He had a darkness that was different from the others. I always suspected that he watched me with cameras, and it seemed that he knew the content of all my texts. It was uncanny; he would show up where I was, or he would know something that had only been sent to me in a private message. He was either extremely intuitive, or somehow knew too much.

I was a different person with each of the men, holding my facades together by a string for nobody but myself.

I was one person on social media.

I was another person with my family.

I was another person with my friends.

I was another person with Bob, Jerry, and Brian.

I was another person to the men offering me money and gifts to join them on trips.

And I was yet another person with myself.

I went on autopilot; most times, I did not want any of it. And in a sense, my true self was nowhere to be found.

Keeping up with all of my different lives started to weigh on me.

When I went over to Brian's, it would be for maybe an hour or less – doing the deed and then leaving.

Jerry and I were playing house. But the lies were growing, along with his resentment and rage. The fights with him became so violent that the police were called multiple times.

He was big, and loud, and scary – and one time, I got hit with an inanimate object that he threw at me in a fit of rage.

Whenever the police came – called by the neighbors – I always said there was nothing wrong and that we were just having a silly argument. Sometimes they would pull me to the side, and say, "Ma'am, are you sure you're okay? Is he violent with you?"

Jerry did not beat me in the traditional sense, but I was scared of making him more angry, so I would say I was fine.

Can I Be Honest? As I take a pause and sit with the enormity of what I was involved in, and the juggling – it is difficult to write this without clenching my fists and feeling a shortness of breath. I have to return to the present moment and gently love on myself.

The lies were filling my mind faster than I could breathe – I had so many personalities showing themselves at different times. My memory is slightly hazy here, since I was still drinking and getting high in order to block out the trauma. But I do know that Jerry was going through my phone and putting the pieces together.

Today, as I think back, I do not blame him for his anger. He put up with a lot, and stayed through two pregnancies that were not his.

I also do not condone his behavior. As I have learned more about trauma, I understand there are different ways that people react to it. Some shut down and stop trusting; others get very, very angry; some dish it back. The trauma went both ways with us. I know I traumatized him with the lies, the promiscuous sex, and the secrecy, and I take full responsibility for my part.

In the midst of the on-and-off of it all, something new and monumental patiently waited for me. My spirit, as dim as it was, begged to be healed.

Meraki [May-Rah-Kee] is doing something with total love, and pure soul. It is leaving a little piece of yourself in your creative work.
- Unknown

I ached to find my passion and purpose. I thought I could possibly sing professionally, and I tried with all my might.

I connected with a renowned drummer, some rappers and some producers. I was not just searching for validation this time. I was actively searching for someone to invest in my career.

But of course, I thought I had to offer my body in exchange. I thought I was useless otherwise. I did not think my voice was good enough unless I tossed that "extra" in there. The truth is, my challenge with musical rhythm and extreme stage fright made it difficult to work with me professionally. I could hardly sing in front of even one or two people without getting so hot and scared that I sometimes would cry and shake within seconds. I don't think anyone ever heard my real voice because of this.

Maybe if I show them my talent in other ways, they will invest the money in order to make me good enough.

Naturally, every attempt at becoming a singer failed, as my mindset was not healthy, nor did it hold any truth. I had a state of mind of such worthlessness that I thought I was incapable of succeeding in any way without a man's support.

I look at my history now and realize how detrimental the long-term entanglement with Bob was. The damaging tape had begun to play for me at 16, in Bob's office.

That tape said, "You must give your body over in order to receive abundance. You will only be able to experience the financial freedom you seek by exploiting your physical appearance." The message was catastrophic, and single-handedly altered the trajectory of my life.

One day, my friend Lee invited me on her family vacation, which happened to be around the time of my birthday. I told her I had not made any plans for my birthday, and she insisted I celebrate with her on the cruise. The destinations were Belize, the Grand Cayman islands, and Honduras. It could not have been a more perfect idea.

The islands hold a deep meaning for me. They represent a combination of liberation, vitality, and joy; and the feeling of the warm sun on my skin is unexplainably wonderful.

My mother used to talk about St. Thomas as her dream destination. When I first googled the photos and saw the blue water, my heart felt like it could explode. I knew that someday, I needed to be there.

So, I had always felt an emotional pull to places with water that blue. When I had a chance to go there with Lee and her family, I took it.

The day before the ship was scheduled to leave the port, Lee and I ran to the mall to grab a couple things for the trip. We were both die-hard leggings fans, and we tried a bunch of them on in popular name-brand stores. Whenever I was in the dressing room, I found myself utterly disappointed in the fit and fabric of the leggings. They were priced at about $120, and I could not understand how they could allow such poor quality leggings in stores, when they were so obviously not worth the price. I had many complaints about them, from the looseness around my ankles, to the ethics of the clothing company, to the way the waistband suffocated me. The overall store experience left me feeling worse when I left than when I walked in.

Don't the owners care that we're experiencing this self loathing in their beautiful and expensive stores? I thought. I shared my opinions with Lee once we sat down for a coffee to take a break from shopping.

"I mean honestly, babe, do you hear me on this? Am I the only one? We just spent $120 on those leggings, and we're not even fully happy. I'm gonna wear 'em, but I'm gonna hate the camel toe the whole time, and probably wear an oversized hoodie to hide that, along with my belly," I said in a clearly frustrated tone.

I was born at almost 10 pounds, with cheeks that looked like I might be saving food in them for later. My belly always had three or more rolls, and my arms were thick as thieves. Growing up, I had a double chin, back fat that detested any elastic, and inner thighs that burned and chafed when I walked for more than five minutes in the heat. It was agonizing to be in my own skin.

My body always seemed to be in the way of my joy. If you had dressed me in a snowsuit in the middle of a heat wave, it might have been a little more pleasant than what I was experiencing back then. I was trying to crawl out of my body, and change it with all my might – except in any healthy way.

I was taking pills like Adderall and snorting cocaine to curb my appetite. I would get in the gym for a week, and then give up quickly. I did not feel comfortable even being there, because I would have to wear gym clothes. And gym clothes did not feel supportive. They seemed to just highlight all the excess.

Lee calmly sipped her coffee and said, "Aren't you living in LA? That's like fashion central. Stop bitching about it, and make the perfect leggings. I'm sure you can find someone to sew. Oh and when you do make them, make me a pair too." I was completely taken aback by the idea.

Me? Make clothes? I still couldn't figure out what my fucking reality was, let alone decide to run a business. But alas, we can do **whatever the fuck** we put our mind to. Lee was right. In LA, I was 30 minutes away from the fashion district and I had friends who could sew.

I ran with the idea. I decided to do some research and find fabrics that looked and **felt** good to me – fabrics that I would want to dress myself in. The first sample I ever tried had me floored. I screamed, I danced, I cried. On that first day, in the piles of fabric that stretched in all directions, I found a material that fit into every crease on my body, and held me in a way that I had been waiting to be held for my whole life.

The material's design and specifications were so unique that I was sure that nothing else on the planet existed like it. I was right; and today, thousands of women who have tried it have not felt anything else like it. At that moment, my clothing company was born – and I found my purpose.

To the naked eye, it all seems fairly simple: leggings, bodysuits, crop tops – in black, white, brown – whatever, right? Nothing you haven't seen before. **Wrong**. You cannot point at a **feeling**; you cannot patent it; you cannot copy it; you cannot name it. It's **Love** – on your body.

I became obsessed with creating clothing. It was what I breathed, ate, dreamed, and hurt over. I have always had an intense reaction to anything about which I am excited or passionate. When it happens, I actually vibrate and feel like I ingested an entire eight-ball of cocaine, even if I am completely sober. It used to freak me out, and everyone else too. Now, as I have learned to integrate and ground, I love this about myself. It is holy.

There was a lot of pain throughout the building process. I had no idea what the future held. But I kept moving forward, because I had found my passion. It was about embracing women and helping them through their greatest personal challenge – the journey of self love. I created physical products that cultivated emotional support and the desire to **Love On** oneself; and I watched year after year as women dropped to their knees in gratitude for my beautiful brand, ***Love On Collections.***

Recently, my mom was with me when I received some samples for a collection that was in the works. She quietly watched as I examined, tried on, huffed and puffed, and held a microscope to every inch of the new pieces.

"I watch you become the fabric, Mima," she said.

And she was right. When it seems like I am not listening or I am obviously mentally elsewhere – it's usually because in my mind, I am inside the fabric, climbing up to the waist of my designs, examining them, thread by thread. Becoming so involved with the fabric and the designs can be borderline unhealthy, because at times it has made me sick and even angry. I have been found laid out in a puddle of tears on the floor. And yet at the same time, the experience is so beautiful because I know it is what makes me feel – deeply. I am fully alive for this art. And for a woman who was numb most of her life, I need that.

I know I am in the divine presence of passion and fire when I am doing this work – creating for the women who need to be held. Initially, I was doing it for myself – but really, it is for all of us. I take this passion into every room; and when a sister tells me how ugly she feels (a sister who turns heads everywhere she goes, by the way) I feel that same fire rising. I feel my heart start to beat more quickly. My eyes gaze deeply into hers, and I take her hand, and I speak whatever words that come to mind – words that might help. I offer all of me to help her see her worth. I want to do anything I can. I will usually cry with her because I can actually feel the pain. The pain of something that once brought me close to death is not a feeling I can forget. The memory causes me to lean even deeper into my purpose.

I became so busy helping other women love on themselves that it still took me years after this new beginning before I fully loved on **me**.

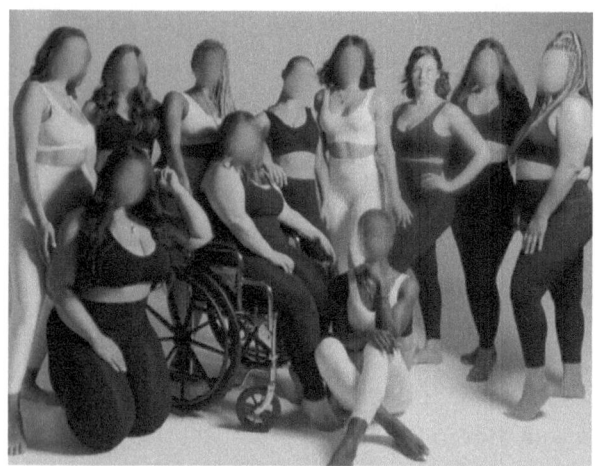

Photoshoot for my first ever collection, 2018

First photoshoot for Collection 27, Los Angeles, 2020

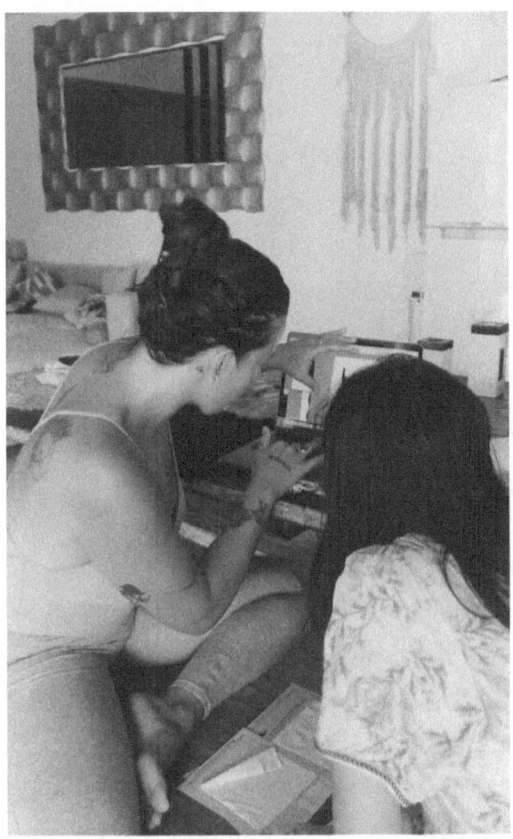

Working on a new collection for Love On in Bali, 2022

The mother of *Love On Collections* was thriving, but my other personas were still alive and well. Remember that I mentioned **two** high-rollers coming into my life? High-roller number two was X, one of Brian's best friends, and someone about whom I had fantasized since I was a teenager. Even though I had run into X on a few separate occasions, I never pursued him, for fear of Brian thinking I would betray him in that way. I did not want to lose my shot at real love with him.

A few years into the growth of *Love On*, I found out that Brian was in a public relationship. He had not told me before I found out, and I was devastated. I had never felt more rejected and worthless. *Why couldn't it be me? I thought. What did I do wrong?*

Obviously, I was dishonest, insecure, pathological, and unequipped to be a partner to anyone. Looking back, I am sure Brian realized that. I sometimes wonder if he knowingly toyed with my instability.

I also quietly give thanks for how the universe protected me from what was not meant for me. At the time, it felt like a devastating rejection; and I might have made myself crazy trying to figure out all the reasons that Brian did not choose me. But today, as I look at it a little deeper, and with a bit more awareness, I have come to realize I was protected and guided in a direction that aligned with my highest good. I am so grateful to have not gone down the path of ending up as his life partner.

At the time, since I was still oblivious to that awareness, I became fixated on Brian's new girlfriend. I wondered what she had that I did not. A blue check on Instagram? A love for Saint Laurent? Perfect makeup and a flat belly? I mentally made lists and obsessed about it for hours.

I felt so flawed and far away from all of that. But then, X reached out to me on Instagram.

At first, I held back and did not respond. I was still trying to stay perfect for Brian, still in full delusion. But X was incredibly persistent. He sent 11 or so messages before I finally responded. I raised an eyebrow and a little devil on my shoulder whispered to me: *You have every reason to indulge in this. You've had a crush on X since you were a kid. Everyone has. This is your chance. Brian just played you, and here you have the notorious X telling you he wants to make you his wife.*

I caved and messaged him back.

We FaceTimed and texted all day for weeks. He said things like, "I really think you're my soul mate," and, "Brian said you were amazing. I don't know why he let you go."

Within the first week of talking, he had a first-class flight booked for me to Dublin. I would meet him there for dinner and attend his show before embarking on his private jet – along with his family – to London.

I was still with Jerry, still with Bob, and still accepting gifts and money for my time with others. My ability to move as though I was only with one man at a time is fascinating to look back at today. I actually believed my own lies; and I was convinced that they, too, believed them.

It was clear that X had put a lot of effort into planning our trip. He had arranged for a private escort to meet me as I exited the plane; then, I was guided in a blacked-out Mercedes to a five-star hotel. That night, he shut down an entire restaurant so we could dine alone, and had a candlelit table placed in the middle, just for us.

Before his concert, we were served drinks and food in his dressing room. I watched as he prayed with his dance crew and hyped himself up to run out into the stadium where thousands awaited him. He designated a security guard for me if I wanted to roam, and reserved a high-level seat near the DJ and his family if I wanted to watch the show.

We stepped into luxurious setting after luxurious setting, where everything we wanted was available to us. Security guards followed us everywhere.

When the cops pulled our car over one night after an elaborate dinner, a quick whisper took place between the driver and officer. Without even a moment in between, another black car pulled up beside us, and X took my hand as we stepped out and discreetly switched vehicles.

At that moment, I felt his power.

When someone took a picture of us – which happened a few times – his guard would go up to them and simply take their phone.

He was protected from every angle.

At an underground, membership-only casino, X spent $750,000 and lost it all on a number I told him to bet. Twenty-nine, my lucky number.

Whoops.

He was completely calm and carried on laughing with his friends.

The rage inside of me was boiling. My family's history of poverty and scarcity made me hyper-aware of waste and excessive spending. I was around that kind of behavior often – and perhaps it was hypocritical of me to not say anything – yet, every time I witnessed it, my stomach turned in knots. I bit my tongue. *Don't they know how much that can help someone? I would ask myself. A small country or ME, MAYBE?*

"I'm just gonna post a picture on Instagram for a brand tomorrow and get that back. All good," he announced to his posse. I contained my anger, and laughed along with the others. Whenever X made a joke or an arrogant comment, I saw his eyes seek others' reactions, expecting laughs and approval. Everyone he had around him was hand-picked, and they all knew that was their role – to please the boy.

I saw and felt how the fame had shaped him into a validation-seeking machine, and how it had turned off, or tucked away, his pure essence.

Reflections.

One night in his penthouse suite, I found myself blabbing. And I **could not** stop. X offered me a Percocet and it only made things worse. I went on and on about how different I was – how much of a minimalist and spiritual woman I was; how turned off I was to clubbing and shopping; and how I was really an innocent homebody.

I started crying **hysterically** when he said:

"Why are you here then, Sarah? I already thought you were different and special. But now that you won't stop going off about it…"

I felt his attraction diminishing and my embarrassment growing, but I kept adding fuel to the fire. Something inside of me wanted to sabotage the experience to the point of no return.

The following night, Brian found out that X and I were together after one of his friends ran into us. The tension in our relationship increased as X and Brian viciously texted back and forth. They were fighting, or talking ill about me, or both. X only told me a little and shared a few of the texts, proving Brian's jealousy. But he hid the rest. I was done there.

Of my last night with X (he made an excuse to cut the trip short), I cannot remember anything. I woke up naked and confused, with a towel falling from my chest (although I was sure we had not had sex the entire trip.) A car was waiting outside the lobby to take me to the airport.

It was one of the most embarrassing moments of my life.

To this day, I do not know exactly what happened that night. A lot of shame and fear wells up inside of me about the whole thing. I always wanted to forget it – or at least remember all of it. But

I can't. For years following the experience, I felt overwhelming anxiety when the events replayed in my mind. So much felt unsettled, unclear, and crushing. The combination of the events left me nauseated. It would take me years to let a thought of that night slip by without a panic attack making me buckle at the knees.

After the experience with X, Brian came back around. I don't exactly know why. If I had to guess, I would say there was ego involved. Men sharing women – one of them not getting what they wanted, the other trying to keep her as a toy.

Am I getting warm?

We never mentioned the fact that Brian now had a girlfriend. I just buried my resentment, and came when called.

He still expressed a deep caring for me, and he would come and spend time with me at my Hollywood apartment, although he would normally never go anywhere without a disguise or security guard – especially since he had a girlfriend. I had my justification: *He needs me as a safe haven – he trusts me.*

Is this even important information, or do I just want it out of my mind and body?

The last few times that he contacted me, Brian was more desperate and drunk than ever. He would call me until I picked up, and then offer me the world if I would come spend a night with him.

Love On breathed life and purpose into me, and though I still had much work to do, I had a steady burning desire to be the woman everyone thought I was, the one who loved and respected herself. I watched as the clothing inspired women to take better care of themselves – and as I witnessed that process, I was inspired to take better care of myself.

The fight within me to break free continued to grow. Sometimes I would find a moment of power within myself and I would say **no** to Brian. But his persistence and manipulation made me give in. "After everything we've been through, you're really going to ignore me when I need a friend? I'll remember this," he would threaten.

I would drop everything, no matter where I was, and run to him. After all my effort and patience, I could not let him think I would not show up for him when he needed me most.

But now, I too had an agenda. I was sick of going home empty-handed, used up and heartbroken. So I agreed to see him for one last hoorah, and I vowed that I would get some serious cash out of it. *He owes me*, I told myself.

I boarded my flight to Vegas, where a car was waiting to take me to meet him at the club. He came around the back, stuck his head in the window and gave me a kiss. He then handed me his hotel key and said, "Go get dressed and meet me back here; the car will wait for you."

It was not often that we were out in public together. Because I was slightly intrigued, I put the key in my pocket and gave him a nod. The car took me off to the Cosmopolitan.

In his suite, I got dolled up for an evening of casino and club bouncing with some of his friends.

We had an extravagant time. I have flashes of $100,000 poker chips in my memory, along with rounds of Hennessy and espresso martinis. I remember passionate kissing in the cars between venues, strip clubs, and a slight glimpse of black lace, right before the lights went out. I woke up at 5 a.m., still drunk. Brian was knocked out.

As I was gathering myself in the bathroom, I noticed his bag of cash – $30,000 in cash and 20 or so $25,000 chips laying beside it. I knew chips were tracked and I would have no way of selling them easily, so I was not interested in those.

But at the casino that night, Brian had leaned over to me and whispered, "Don't worry, I'm gonna make sure you leave with some wins too, baby." I had looked at him with a piercing low gaze, and said, "Minimum $30,000." We clinked glasses.

"I got you," he said while still holding my gaze.

So, when I saw the bag in the bathroom, and him asleep in the bed, I decided to just take it.

I figured that he would text me later and I would remind him of the conversation. We had been going for years at this point, so I felt comfortable with my decision.

I pulled up to the rental car place around 6 a.m. I knew I couldn't get on a plane with that much cash, so I decided to drive back home.

The only car they had left was a black Camaro. *How appropriate*, I thought.

As I settled into the rental car, Brian sleepily FaceTimed me. With a note of confusion in his voice, he asked me, "Did you see what I did with my chips?"

I smirked, and said, "Nah, I just took the cash."

"Shit, OK. My drunk ass lost like $200,000 in chips. I'll call you back," he mumbled. Click.

Goodbye, Brian.

As the sun was coming up, I sped off through the desert with that bag of cash in the passenger seat, music blasting.

I took a deep breath and felt a rush of gratitude for the sunrise and the cool breeze. I was done with that life.

I knew that a great deal of healing would be required. Once I began, serious shifts occurred.

I was invited to my first women's weekend retreat, in Lake Tahoe. While reading the itinerary, I saw "Mushroom Ceremony" and quickly looked up to meet the gaze of the facilitator. "I'm happy to join in on everything but **that**," I said in a serious tone.

My traumatic experiences with psychedelics still stuck to me like lint to leggings. I remembered hospital visits from getting drugged with PCP, and suicide attempts when I took too many mushrooms.

No, thanks. I am too emotionally sensitive to take psychedelics. I am too crazy and have too many fears and demons. They are not for people like me, I thought; I had been repeating that to myself for years. I then proceeded to tell a version of that story to the facilitator of the retreat.

She stayed steady and quiet for a moment, and then responded with her hand on mine.

"We can rewrite that together. When done in an intentional and safe space, psilocybin is one of the most powerful medicines on this planet. I encourage you to face your fear and know that you are exactly where you need to be. We've got you. It will be a small dose, and you are surrounded by support."

Her words resonated with me, and I decided to stay open to the idea.

I am glad I stayed open. Plant medicine would be a major factor in breaking me free from depression, trauma, and anxiety. Mushrooms, specifically, were my parachute. They brought me down safely from my reckless life, lovingly guiding me home.

That has been my personal experience, and I in no way intend to sway anyone's opinions. But it truly was, and still is, one of the most profound experiences of my life. I microdose, or take tiny doses, daily; and I feel my focus sharpen, my mood lighten, and my clarity heighten.

The book *How to Change Your Mind* by Michael Pollen was a huge eye-opener for me. It shines light on the reason why mushrooms were made illegal in the first place; and explains the science behind the way they assist in healing depression, anxiety, PTSD, and much more.

The first mushroom ceremony was absolutely beautiful. I took just one gram, which to most people is hardly enough to take you on a whole journey. But the truth is, I **am** sensitive, and I needed a more controlled dose. I also needed to set some intentions in order to reap the benefits of that magical medicine.

I told the room of 12 women about Bob and about a lot of my shame. My words were received with so much love, and I felt lighter when I left – like another outer layer was peeled off, helping me to get closer to my true self. I knew I was going to make some big moves soon in order to shed my old ways.

A few weeks later, I had my own ceremony at home in my Hollywood penthouse. I don't know what compelled me to take psilocybin at home alone on a Tuesday afternoon, but I did – and I immediately panicked. I called a friend who was also a ceremony facilitator and asked her to come save me. I told her that I was not OK, and that something was wrong.

She responded gently, and encouraged me to breathe deeply and slowly. I will never forget what she said that led me to let go and have one of the most powerful awakenings I have ever had.

"**You** are the medicine, Sarah. You don't need anyone to come save you anymore."

I got off the phone, put on some high-vibrational music and started moving my body.

Within 20 minutes, I was crying hysterically. I had snot dripping down my face onto my shirt and I was on my knees, looking up into the sunlight beaming through the floor-to-ceiling windows.

My weeping was coming from a place so ancient and deep that I did not recognize the sounds coming from within me. I was sobbing loudly, and talking passionately to God.

The experience, if I can put it into words, was a brawl between **light** and **dark**.

The medicine was showing me the battle I had been fighting inside myself. It came down to a choice: did I want to choose the light, or let the darkness take me?

My physical experience reflected a true inner war. I was pulling at my shirt, begging to be let go, gasping for air. I wailed, "Please, please," while thrashing about. I was feeling both sides pulling me in different directions.

Which one was I going to choose?

This went on for about two hours, and when I finally released the fight and chose, I was crying tears of joy – tears of triumph. I felt as though I had won a war. I **fought** for the light.

Shortly after the magnificent gift of that experience, I released Bob. It was at the 10-year mark since we had begun. It happened very naturally and easily; which is ironic, considering that I always thought I was trapped and unable to leave. It had been 10 years of lies – 10 years of selling my body – and 10 years of darkness.

When the COVID-19 pandemic hit, Bob reached out with a text to tell me he could not afford the same amount of money he had been sending me every month. He said that he thought he could perhaps send half as much. I felt a sigh of relief, even though I did not know how I would be able to afford to live at my current standard.

Then I did something I had never done before.

I did not respond to him.

As I write this, it has been about three years since that text was sent.

Not too long after I ushered Bob out of my life, I also ended things with Jerry. Then, I swiftly moved out of my Hollywood penthouse. I sold my Jeep Wrangler – a car that I'd had since my New York days, carrying all the dust of my dirty deeds – and moved into a small studio beach cottage in San Diego, along with my dog.

I soon realized how truly uncomfortable I had been in such a large apartment in LA. I knew deep down that the only reason I ever moved into such a place was to prove to myself that I was capable of manifesting it.

Finally, I was over the glamor – and more disgruntled by it than ever. I was ready to cultivate a lifestyle that aligned with my authentic values – qualities like minimalism, simplicity and cleanliness. I began stripping down, while gearing up to peer under my many masks.

I started reading a lot. I spent days and days alone. I cooked, and frequently walked to the park with my dog. I grew *Love On*, and actually started making the most money I had ever made on my own. That was a big one for me, because there was a time when I thought I would never be self-sufficient.

Before long, I hardly saw anyone from my Hollywood life anymore; and when I did, it was a reminder that it was not for me. But everything **was not** perfect. I slipped up a handful of times. For example, after weeks of solitude, I invited Jerry to my cottage. After he got his fill and rolled over, I watched my spirit squirm. I asked myself, "Did you need another reminder?" He then left, leaving me orgasm-less and ashamed.

There were countless days where I would lay in bed watching Netflix, ordering takeout for every meal. Behind closed blinds, I would cry, and feel pathetic and consumed with anxiety. I would wonder what I was doing.

Spending days alone **and** aware was **agonizing**.

I did not realize it then, but that is exactly what healing looks like.

Over the years of sharing my journey with others, women have frequently asked me when it all changed for me. I still don't know how to answer that question. There were so many corners that needed attention. Naturally, fixing one hole in the wall, or emptying one closet, or wiping down one counter does not mean that the house is ready for a showing.

If you are still with me at this point, you might have whiplash from all the back-and-forth. Profound experiences and breakthroughs occurred more times than I can count – and it was still embarrassing that I still was not completely changed. I sometimes would have a streak of a couple weeks – or a maximum of a month – of changed behavior, but I fell back numerous times.

I used to berate myself about it, feeling helpless and like a failure. I would take 10 steps back after making many graceful gazelle-like leaps forward. I could not understand it.

Today, I am grateful for the delays, the setbacks, the relapses, and blockades. It was my training – a priceless education and a concentrated preparation for a life beyond my wildest dreams. I see it all as having been necessary; my foundation was in the process of being restructured. I was putting in my "10,000 hours."

> **The 10,000-hour Rule**
> It takes 10,000 hours of deliberate practice to achieve mastery of something.

I needed to hit the same walls – over and over and over again – until I knew those walls so well that every inch was covered and understood. Every lesson that those walls taught me was learned. And each wall had many, many lessons. During each lesson, I learned another emotional language. I found a little bit more of my own voice, or how to communicate in a healthy manner with a different type of person.

Eventually, I was able to connect with anyone and with everyone, no matter how different our backgrounds. Eventually, all the walls that separated me from my essence came down, and I found an intricate understanding of how inherently loved we all are – how **perfect** we all are.

Eventually, I found an opening to divinity and infinite joy. I found that I could share information with anyone, through verbiage or energy. I could tell my story for **a reason**, not just to hear the sound of my own voice, or to receive validation.

My "10,000 hours" looked like trying different styles of a morning yoga practice until I found my own. It looked like letting go of my **old** story, the old tape, the one that I had become obsessed with telling: **"I am fucked up because this happened to me. I am unworthy because this is how all men treat me. I am crazy. I am unable to receive love. I have trust issues. I fall off every time. I can't commit. I always meet the same type of person. They always end up being bad for me. I hate my job. My life is hard. I don't make enough money. It never works. I am broken."**

Letting go of that programming was revolutionary for me. New neural pathways were energized as I began to input new information in place of the old: **"I am worthy to receive everything I've ever wanted. I am abundant in countless ways. I am always guided, protected, and safe. I am creative."**

And so on. I repeated those affirmations – and more – in different ways, day in and day out. I felt them in my body and I experienced days of deep gratitude and joy.

My morning practice – whether I was doing a 5 minute meditation or writing a gratitude list or simply taking a few conscious breaths with a smile on my face before stepping out of bed – was something that changed many times, but it kept me grounded regardless of any changes. It did not have to always be done the same way, or take the same amount of time. I just had to show up for it – and it repaid me, tenfold. It was imperative to me that I felt what **I** needed to feel, and what my body required. Honoring cycles became the key – resting when the seasons did. I would take it more slowly or pick up the pace, depending on what my hormones requested.

My dog, Sasha, really kept me sane. And when I discovered tech-free days – a concept I learned from Tiffany Shlain's book, *24/6: The Power of Unplugging One Day a Week* – she became my companion in the silence.

For years, I had maintained several social media accounts with large followings. I would obsessively open and close each tab, to check who was liking, commenting, and reposting. It became compulsive. Sometimes I would just scroll without realizing why I was doing it in the first place. My hands would be vibrating and I would start biting my nails, or picking my skin. I knew it was unhealthy; my body's reactions told me it was.

So I started shutting off my phone for a full 24 hours – Friday night to Saturday night. It did not have to be those particular days, but that was what worked for my schedule and flow.

Even aside from social media, I realized how accessible I had made myself. For years, I had always responded to every call – quite literally. It was time to unplug from that. My new practice of taking time for myself with a tech-free day became something I needed, like one might need their morning coffee.

Once I got high off of the liberation and peace that my tech-free days offered, I never went back. I would log off my phone around 5 p.m., and have an entire evening, morning, and day of absolutely nothing, and nobody needing me but myself. What a **treat**. I would cook, nap, stare at the ceiling, draw, and sing. I walked a lot with Sasha. We would walk past the stores and side roads, past the food trucks, and past the kids eating ice cream with their parents and friends.

I really got to know myself. It was slightly surreal, and sometimes I felt like I was an invisible energy with no obligation other than to observe. I noticed all of the things that I had seen before, but now I was really present in a new way. I would stop at the park, and while Sasha played around, I stretched and moved. People stared at me – a lot. I knew it was odd to see a woman alone doing headstands in the middle of a park where people were barbecuing or walking, but I did not care. For me, part of the newness was **being** – being who I wanted to be; doing what felt good for **me**; allowing myself that time; creating a space for true reflection. It was the type of work that resulted in colossal benefits for my mental health.

I practiced feeling uncomfortable when people stared, and it was extra-challenging because I didn't have my phone; I couldn't distract myself. I just had to breathe with the emotions.

When I would log back online on Saturday night, the serenity would be palpable. The urge to scroll was diminished, and the week following would be more peaceful. This was the first practice with which I became 100 percent consistent; and to this day it is still the most important influence on my mental clarity and self-care.

It goes without saying that there were countless setbacks; but there were countless days of pleasure, high frequency, and peace, too. There were weeks at a time where I took wonderful care of myself, watched the sunset with a smile splashed across my face, and ate dinner happily unaccompanied. If I was lucky, I would have dinner with my new neighbor, Toni.

Toni is a genuine, highly intelligent, and benevolent woman. She lived in the cottage across from mine, and soon she became a safe place for me. She would take care of my dog when I was at the gym or working, and would make me coffee in the morning. Sometimes we would watch a movie together;

sometimes she would listen to my fears and dreams and stories, and share insights with me. I watched her become the caretaker for her best friend, who was dying of cancer – and my love for her grew.

A special kinship was formed in our little secluded cottage community. She is about 30 years older than I am, but nevertheless, my friend. I see her as one of the angels that kept me going. I don't think she knew how important it was to have her near at that time.

*If you are at all present for your life,
it will break your heart.*
- Jessica Alix Hesser

I was sharing myself openly and often with my family and social media community, cleaning up messes I had made over the years. Yet, little bits and pieces of my life remained that still needed attention – bits around men, mostly.

My journey was painfully slow; and the unraveling, as you have learned if you have gotten this far, was not linear.

I hit a plateau with *Love On*, and multiple setbacks discouraged me. When clothing production was paused, I would make some money through a website that paid me to post pictures of myself. They were not fully nude, but they went just far enough to still fall into the category of exploiting my physical appearance for cash. I would be lying if I said I didn't know what the recipients were doing with those pictures.

Again, I was faced with another form of sabotage. I might have been done with this man or that man, but I still could not put my full trust in my **own** ability to generate abundance **without** men.

That said, I feel it is important to note that I have no qualms with women who choose that life. I hold no judgment. My personal story and truth is: that way of living was abusive to **my** soul. If it is not that way for you, that's OK, and I celebrate whatever brings you true joy and empowerment. After everything I had been through, though, it was imperative for me to walk away from that life in order to meet myself and experience my full potential.

It was painful to work on personal growth and step away from things that did not serve me, while still operating from a place of fear, and still feeling lost.

I decided to take a trip to look for some answers. Isn't that funny? I still thought the answers were somewhere outside of myself!

While in Costa Rica for a short time, I met a man who disguised himself as the possible "man of my dreams." Now I can see that the flags were as red as they could get, and that I was settling. But he seemed to have **some** of the things on my list. You know what list I'm talking about, don't you? The list that names all the qualities that your dream partner should have? *My dream man is: healthy, tall, kind, etc.*

My list had changed over the years. Things were added or removed as certain things became clearer to me and others less important. Be that as it may, I was not **fully** being the woman who would meet the man on that list. **That** woman would not take calls from her toxic ex. That woman would not gallivant abroad with a struggling musician, paying for all his meals and accommodations while he was out having sex with other women. She definitely would not have sex with that same man, who liked to **physically hurt her** as a turn-on.

No, **that** woman would **never**.

That woman would walk with a posture that demanded respect. She would not define her worth by her relationship status or lack thereof. She would know – and would have at the forefront of her mind – that it is her **birthright** to experience honest, uplifting, pleasurable, reciprocal and supportive love. Nothing would take that away from her.

That woman would tell the truth in every instance, because she was safe in her own being. She would never keep her feelings inside just to please a man. **That** woman's walk would tell you that she knew herself, and also that she would never lower her frequency to meet others in their negativity. **That** woman would effortlessly lift **them** to meet her in her "highness."

And of course, she would be kind and gentle as she addressed the struggling musician; but she would most definitely deliver a message of "No, thank you," not "Please come in and take all of me."

But I had not fully embodied **that** woman yet. So I had to keep learning.

John was broke, without a pot to piss in – my favorite type of man. We had met through a family member, and when he heard I was staying in Costa Rica for a while, he reached out to me. I sent him my number and we began messaging back and forth about our travel plans. I quickly offered up the couch in my Airbnb, not realizing that we would – without hesitation – share a bed upon his arrival.

We spent about two months hopping from one Airbnb to another, on the western edge of Costa Rica's Nicoya Peninsula. There sat a famous yet tiny beach town known as Santa Teresa.

The entirety of Santa Teresa was just one long road, creating an unavoidable habit of running into the same people every day if you stayed there. The town – we just referred to it as "Santa" – attracted surfers and yogis from all over the world. It was easy to find a community of like-minded individuals there; we couch-surfed, danced, and spent endless hours on the beautiful beaches. Every day, I would throw on a bikini and ride on the dirt roads on an ATV through the luscious, humid jungles. The countryside was filled with monkeys, lizards, and waterfalls.

It was truly "pura vida," an expression that Costa Ricans use to describe their free, natural, laid-back lifestyle. Each day was an adventure. I met some wonderful people – and even made a best friend while walking down the street my first week there.

Harmony Sunshine is her name, and we were inseparable. Harmony is a vibrant, pure and talented artist. Her face is what I imagined a baby angel would look like once grown up, and her body is shaped like a goddess's – big hips, tiny waist, and long golden locks that reach her perfectly-curved lower back. She is a word-play genius with a voice that gathers the birds and bees in its tones. Her eyes have the forest, the ocean and the moon inside of them.

And – I discovered that she was the only one I had ever known that **got** my sense of humor. I was never letting her go.

Harmony and me in Costa Rica

So it was Harmony and her partner, and John and I who would go everywhere together. Our gang quickly grew to six with a couple more wonderful additions that we picked up along the way. We stayed in decorated villas, cooked delicious dinners together, played chess by the pool (well, I watched as they played), and took in the electrifying sunsets on the rooftops. All the while, the boys serenaded us with their acoustic guitars.

The truth still lay under the beauty of what surrounded me. I was in Costa Rica searching for something, but I was repeating old patterns. I avoided facing the elephant in my life – inauthenticity. I was still running, still involved with abusive and flaky men, and I was neglecting my business back in LA that was seemingly falling apart due to my fears. I went to Costa Rica intending to search deeply, but found myself filling the void inside me with my old vices of submissive sex and delusion. I was trying to convince myself that John was my person, and all my energy was going towards that.

This was not a new experience, really. I almost always started such an entanglement. I would pour my entire being into a new man's cup until it runneth over. During the first couple weeks of a relationship, I would usually think, *He might be the one*, no matter who it was.

There is an old children's book called *Are You My Mother?* by P.D. Eastman, where a young bird walks around searching for her mother, asking every animal that she encounters if it might be her. My mother and I joke about that book now, saying that it is how we evaluated men – "Are you my soulmate? Are you? Are you?" We would ask that about each man as we hopped from one relationship to the next. Essentially, I was undertaking a relentless search to find the man who would **"complete me."** Today, I know that kind of thinking is a scam.

Both people in a relationship must show up 100 percent; otherwise, toxicity is unavoidable. We cannot heal wounds that are not our own to heal. My understanding is that we cannot be completed, saved, or healed by another. However, there are those who come into our lives to heal **bits** – or, they may teach us lessons that shake us to the core, and push us to become better.

To feel as though you are constantly in search of another half is telling yourself that you are not capable of experiencing love from within. You are telling yourself that you cannot be your own medicine. It comes from a belief that you are not worthy of the experience that is love. And if you cannot feel love, in your own presence, you will be forever searching – showing up halfway for someone as they show up halfway for you. The love that's missing in your life is not that of a lover's – it is your own.

In Costa Rica, my episodes of depression were fewer, but still frequent. A major factor in those episodes was the skin on my face; I had vicious acne for years. And there were other symptoms that frustrated me, like brain fog, short-term memory loss, sharp breast pain, shallow breathing, and anxiety.

One night, in the midst of waves of emotion, I found myself in a treehouse on my hands and knees, praying to God.

I had been out and about, enjoying my time in Santa; but I was also hiding underneath makeup, avoiding looking at people straight-on. I did not want them to see my flared jawline; I was constantly putting my hair in front of my face to cover the cystic and inflamed marks on my jaw, neck, and chin. It was not only physically painful, but it also hurt my spirit. I felt that I had to hide when I was dying to dance and play. I wanted to be able to look up at the sun, feel it kiss my face, and not drop my neck in shame as I remembered what people would see if I kept my chin stretched.

To counteract my depression, I had been utilizing tools and teachings from all the work I had done in San Diego, and from all the books I had read and courses I had taken. So I pushed through and practiced my affirmations, conducted plant medicine ceremonies, willed the negative thoughts away, meditated and journaled, and ate extremely healthy.

But that night in the treehouse, I crumbled, and asked God why I still had marks on my face. I knew that I had done everything right! Everything I consumed was fresh, local, and nutritious. I got plenty of sun, spent time in nature, laughed a lot, and exercised every day. I did not eat dairy, or soy; and I drank plenty of water. Sure, I still had toxic men in my life sometimes, but that doesn't give you acne – does it?

I did genuinely question myself about that last point, and wondered if my choice in men might have contributed to the acne – even slightly?

After crying, pleading, and listing (out loud) all the things I had done in order to heal the acne, I went to bed with puffy eyes and a light whimper.

The next day, while scrolling through my phone, I came across an article about a woman who swore that the removal of her breast implants had healed all of the unexplainable symptoms of illness she had. Her biggest symptom was cystic acne.

My eyes widened. I had never heard about that connection before. I had heard about – and tried – all the lasers, products, diets, and herbs, but no one had ever suggested that something foreign inside of me might need to be explanted. I determinedly continued my research for hours, and found communities of women online who also claimed their acne symptoms were alleviated following explant surgery. My body was responding with excitement and joy. I felt that this was the truth; my solution.

Before scheduling the surgery, I had a talk with myself. I decided that I was going to go forward with it, regardless of whether it was the cure for the acne or not. I already had been in the process of undoing the damage that some other artificial enhancements had done to my hair, hormones, psyche, eyelashes, nails, and skin. I made the decision to have surgery knowing that – no matter what happened with the acne after the procedure – I was ready to drop the fakery and meet my authenticity in every way.

I quickly found a US board-certified surgeon in San Jose, Costa Rica, and took a small plane there four days later. My mother flew out to care for me, post-surgery – and my friends helped too, once I returned to the villa in Santa Teresa.

Since it would take me a minimum of four weeks to heal and I was advised to avoid sweating, I did not do much other than spend time in the villa. Sweating, I was told, could cause a dangerous infection in the incision areas. Yet, truthfully, I did not mind an uneventful convalescence. I have always enjoyed a quiet place in the center of nature. I loved waking to the sounds of the roosters crowing and birds chirping; and I was enjoying my gigantic air-conditioned living room. During my recovery, I journaled, lightly stretched, sang, and cooked.

The gang would go out to the beach and do other fun activities, and I would stay back to care for my new body.

Very quickly, my breathing became lighter, yet fuller. I was mystified – and grateful to feel my natural breasts for the first time in seven years. I felt like myself again.

The acne did not disappear entirely. Afterall, the implants had done damage during those seven years, and I now needed to be patient and trust the healing.

It would take about a year before the full changes occurred, but I did my part in letting my body meet itself again. I stopped all unnatural practices, from hair dying, to applying acrylic nails and false lashes, and more. I watched my body take its natural shape as my real breasts dropped into place and the fat from the Brazilian butt lift all those years ago started transferring and reabsorbing back into my body. I dropped weight due to swimming and exercising, and all of a sudden, I recognized my reflection. A natural lifestyle, including yoga, allowed for a gentle return to myself.

And slowly, I disentangled from John. I did not end it right away, but I felt myself growing more and more distant from him. And found that I was less attracted to him.

During my last days in Santa, I was hit with an enormous wave of inspiration to design a new collection for *Love On*. I daydreamed for hours and coordinated the photoshoots, models, marketing, and color palettes while I packed and booked my travel arrangements back to California.

John was to stay a while longer, couch-surfing and hitchhiking.

After about a month or so, I went to visit him.

While at an Airbnb in Florida with John for a few days, I noticed his desire to inflict physical harm during sex escalating. He wanted to hit me in the face, and I allowed for it – even pretending like it turned me on, too. It was a dark game and I did not fully grasp what was happening the first times we played it. I had not yet stepped into radical honesty, which meant I smiled easily and took it, even though my whole body was screaming for it to stop. My facial reactions and verbiage gave him permission. It was a talent I had – putting on an excellent show out front when backstage was an absolute disaster.

After so many years of degradation and abuse, my body found autopilot in those moments, and I went into character.

"Be what he wants you to be" was a mantra that I had been repeating day in and day out, but I was not aware of it. I was casting spells in my mind, unaware of the damage it was doing and how long it would really take me to heal from it all.

The last time I saw John was at the beginning of the development process for the new Love On collection, which has always been a very difficult time for me. As an introvert in an industry like mine, I feel the stress of the challenge, and my emotional stability does get shaken.

The few days that he stayed with me were enough to tell me what I needed to know – this was not my person. We barely spoke, and I just wanted him to leave.

After he left, I fell apart at the seams. My emotions thundered inside and around me, and I felt a complete loss of life. I know now that my body was speaking to me, and showing me the havoc that is wreaked when we give ourselves over to someone for their thrill.

When we do that, our bodies become diseased, our pH balances are thrown off, our tears flood, and our worth is put into question. That goes for both men and women. When the sex is not a full "yes," our bodies and emotions will let us know.

I was distraught. I did not know why, since I was still disconnected from my body, and I could not hear what she was telling me. It was like seeing blood, and then feeling the panic rise when you cannot find where the wound is, or from where the blood is pouring.

I went backward 10 years. To a great degree, I was that same 17-year-old girl in that hotel room, wanting to take my life after a man walked out full – and me, empty. Once again, I was sick with the sight of my own reflection, and the pain saturated my every crevice. I lay choking on my tears, shocked that I was there – again.

I was at a point in my journey where – thankfully – I had a community of women to whom I could reach out; these were women who specialized in healing the body and mind. I had taken part in several plant medicine ceremonies, and had tried a handful of methods and modalities, courses, herbs, and coaches.

But I was desperate too, and Briana could feel it when I sent her a voice note. To me and many other people, Reverend Briana Lynn, simply put, is a powerful woman, with incredible abilities to help people move out of dark places and on with their lives. I had not worked with her one-on-one, but had been blessed to know her through ceremonies and family gatherings.

She has a way with words. She is a channel and a vessel. Any time she speaks, it is as if something or someone is speaking through her. I knew I could reach out to Briana even though we had not spoken recently. She would know what to do.

I was lying in the bathtub, my sunken shoulders heaving from a weep so deep that it had come from the core of my belly and shook my bones. I grabbed my phone from the floor and sobbed into it, asking Briana to help guide me to my healing. I told her I did not know what to do anymore. I asked her why I was still stuck – why I still found myself wanting to die – why I could not get away from the sadness and vicious cycles, even after all the healing I had done. I wanted so badly to shed this pattern that had gracelessly undone me a thousand and one times.

Briana did not give me my answers. It was not because she lacked the knowledge; and it was not because she did not say what I needed to hear. It was because I found the way myself when I simply uttered those words into the phone. I had stopped pretending that I had it all handled. I succumbed at that moment – and it was remarkable.

The universe is kind to us when we are unambiguous and devoted to growth. It is generous when we make it clear that we want to go higher, and that we are willing to do the work. It sends us little bursts of energy – or a random phone call – or a butterfly – or a sunset view – something that just reminds us how precious it all really is.

The next morning, I signed up for two women's courses, to be held via Zoom calls. One had been suggested by Briana, and the other by Yasmeen, another incredible teacher. Both courses, which would not start until the next week, were like lights in a dark room for me. Just by knowing I had done something to choose myself, I felt the energy start to flow back into my veins.

While still rattled and tender, I got on the first Zoom calls and introduced myself to the combined 35 women in the courses. I felt my body belonging there with them, and the words that flowed from me were potent and honest.

To get me out of the house, my girlfriend invited me to dinner at a place with an ocean view – and I got a breath of fresh air. I started getting up at 5 a.m. and meditating regularly again. I was reinvigorated, and I knew that if I just kept going like that, I might see the other side. The despair from the week before had already faded from my thoughts.

On every day that followed, I did the spiritual work that I needed to do, and I was enthralled with the results and my energy level. Briana taught me the true definition of radical honesty, and I became spellbound by its potential. Every unhealthy tie or entanglement faded gracefully out of my life – and I was, for the first time, completely devoid of toxic relationships.

Truth consumed my thoughts. My mind craved learning all the ways that I could become acquainted with it. It was like meeting someone you wanted to learn everything about, and then making it a point to get every detail absolutely perfect. I fell in love with what the truth made me feel about myself.

I also became very clear about what my place was in the spiritual community, and for what I stood. I felt like I had a foot in two worlds. The New Age spiritual community has a lot of beauty, but also a lot of facade to it. I started feeling very out of place – like I was not "spiritual enough" for the New Agers – yet, I seemed "too spiritual" to fall in with mainstream ideologies. Where did **I** fit in? What was **my** sect?

It took me a little while, but I realized that I belong to no specific community. I am my own twist on things, and my spiritual practice involves just being a good, decent human. I work on that, and do what feels right for me. I bring a rawness into the spiritual rooms that need it, and I can bring a wholesome point of view to the mainstream. I am for everyone and for no one. I have had a taste of what it looks like to be completely over on one side or the other, and so I choose a healthy balance.

Now, I do not care about how many ecstatic dance parties or sound baths you go to. *Do you consider other people's time?*

I do not care at all if you consistently sit in ayahuasca ceremonies or walk barefoot in fields. *Can I finish my thought without you interrupting?*

It matters very little if you speak a spiritual language and throw words around like "manifesting" or "sacred" or "flowing." *Can I trust you with my range of emotions? Do you speak lovingly to your parents? Do you give people a heads-up if you are going to be late?*

You can sit Indian-style with incense burning all day if you'd like, it makes no difference to me.

If you eat plants and use all-natural products, but hiss at the customer service representative... Are you really living clean?

Does your family receive very little love and time from you, yet you offer it freely to those on social media and at social events?

Do you post quotes on social media about loyalty, and respect, and non-judgment – but then gossip about what others choose to do with their own bodies and lives?

I started peeling back these layers of spirituality so I could taste the nectar and lick the roots of the things that truly contribute to making this a more peaceful, loving world.

As I continued to study and learn, I slowly came down from what the beginning of a spiritual journey almost always includes – a high horse.

*The world cannot ruffle the dignity
of a soul that dwells in its own tranquility.*
- John O'Donohue

Topanga Canyon in all of its sweetness, 2022...

It's late Saturday morning in the canyon and I bring my knees close to my chest, creating a slanted but impermeable table for my journal to rest on. I inhale – and audibly exhale – the scent of sauteing onions that is traveling from the kitchen to the guest room where I stay, and I feel a gentle chill breeze down my arm. It's not cold outside, but the air-conditioning and the glass french doors generously showcase majestic nature with its perfectly-paced raindrops, and in my mind, it's late autumn falling into winter.

I hear nothing but Yasmeen's father shuffling about gracefully in the kitchen. He is making breakfast for us, and it's absolute music to my ears. My phone sits buried in my suitcase, powered off, unresponsive to the outside turbulence that tries to overpower and consume me. The city in all of its uproar and hustle is only two-and-a-half miles down the road, but if you asked me where I am, I would say I'm abroad in a mountainous utopia.

I create these pockets of peace for myself, knowing I must re-enter into the world of constant pings very soon. But after years of practicing this freedom from interference – shutting down once a week – I know I will step back into the noise with a **hush** and a steadiness. It will be felt and noticed, in myself and in others. "What's her secret?" people ask, puzzled, as if it's something completely beyond them.

A lover's hand tracing a long ignored vein tucked behind your knee can show you where you hide your sorrow. A knot in your shoulder when pressed just so can bloom into information about your frustrations. But there are also shapes and postures we can only achieve when we are being held – or constrained – by other bodies and other places. There are locations with precise geometric intelligence that as they contain you, change you. Suddenly, like a caterpillar curled in the chrysalis, you are safe enough to finally melt. Contained, embraced by form with enough security, that you can risk a previously unimaginable transformation.

- Sophie Strand from The Container

After some time of committing to myself and not having anyone enter me, a deep desire for a true partnership and a sacred union started churning. I had never been in a real relationship; obviously, all the ones I'd had before – no matter how loving some moments seemed – were all a lie in one way or another.

I began to truly learn the rhythm of my body, and for the first time in my life, I bled on the same day every month. I even synced up with the full moon – which, in my book, was proof that my body was coming back online. After all the womb trauma I had endured, and all the abuse I had allowed on my most sacred parts, I was finally rising from my descent.

As I fearlessly shared – and emptied – my lifelong suitcase of falsehoods, I became aware of an inner knowing that I am here to love. Something in me knew that the way to find that love was to simply **be** love, in any way possible – and that I should serve through loving. Love would not be achieved by going on a dating app and looking for it – and it would not involve "hooking up" with random strangers until I found it. It would be celebrating other people's relationships and loves. It would be giving an extra big smile and a compliment to the lady at the cash register; and it would include cooking and dancing with myself.

Sometimes, love was laughing with my roommates until my belly hurt, or crying with my brother. Other times, it would be felt by letting myself feel all my feelings, in my room, alone. Then by sharing them with the people who wanted to listen and learn with me, either on social media or in song circles. There was no judgment – all would be embraced for who they were.

Often, love was putting myself aside to hold another woman who needed to be held. Sometimes, that woman was my own mother.

Other times, love was walking through the forest with no phone, or up a hill in the mountains. Or, I would feel it when blasting a love song that shook my bones. I felt a certainty that love was present, and that a king was on his way to meet me in my celebration of life.

I think that the universe is very generous. It just asks us to do our part – to try. The universe does not require perfection, but rather ambition. You do not have to be flawless, but persistent – persistent with the truth of **you**. Who do you want to **be**?

I began with that question. And I began embodying the traits that the higher or best version of myself possesses. I would ask myself: *Am I healthy? Graceful? Patient? Organized? Kind? Generous? Grounded? Radically honest? Healthy in food and in all things consumed? I can be those things now, can't I? If I choose? All of those things are free, and I can do them from anywhere.*

*So why not begin, now, to step into this person I know I can become? It is a process of **becoming**, after all. I have to get the **be** part down.*

I met Christopher in the midst of this time of questioning and self-definition, and I did not recognize him as "the one" right away. Though he "checked all the boxes," I did not take inventory. He was one of my brother's best friends, and well-known eye candy. At 6'5", he has golden hair and eyes so blue and muscles so defined, you might mistake him for your favorite celebrity crush. But, I thought, *that's just Christopher, an obvious shapeshifter.*

When he walked, we would do a double-take, certain he was dancing. It was clear why every woman tried something with him at some point. None got any farther than a kiss.

Christopher had been celibate for 10 months when I first met him on a commune in Pacific Palisades, California. He was visiting from Hawaii, on a quest for self-discovery and full healing.

Our first encounter was a simple and stiff hug. It surprised me, not in a good way, because after hearing all this "sexy" talk about him, I thought his hug might be a little bit warmer. It was quick, dry; and right away I brushed off the thought that he might be anything extraordinary. Initial hugs have always been important to me.

Since he was in town for a while, he joined a group of us on a weekend retreat in Ojai, California. A friend of mine was extremely interested in him, telling me a lot about how they had cuddled and stargazed the first night of the retreat, and how she felt a powerful connection. The loyal woman that I was took that information as a sign that my brother's insinuations (that Christopher and I were meant for each other) could not be true – no matter what the stars said.

Chris and I kept our distance from each other, but something was starting to happen. I had never been in this position – curious, but burying it; disinterested, but gravitating toward. When I entered a room, I found myself searching for him; and when he would walk in, my insides froze with excitement. It did not make sense. I told myself to control those feelings, that maybe it was old stuff arising – "boy crazy" stuff. Nothing of importance or truth.

We carpooled back to Pacific Palisades together, alone for the first time on an hour-long ride. We shared bits of our self-discovery journeys, laughing, and munching on road-trip snacks. I accepted the fact that he was involved with someone else, and that I needed to practice having nonsexual friendships with men.

In the weeks following, I spent more time than usual at the commune. I joined the group in song circles and family dinners, and enjoyed visits with my brother, who lived there ... Christopher, too.

There was a magnetic current bursting between us. If he was sitting in the back, eating crackers, I would leave the group to sit by his side. When my brother mentioned that they were playing music in a yurt, I raced over, just to be present. Christopher and I did not say much to each other; I just felt the need to be near.

One night during a song circle, I had to leave in a rush. Without thinking, I turned and hugged Christopher and no one else. When I left, I could not stop thinking about how odd it was that I did that. My brother and friends were all there, too.

One night, my girls and I all went to dinner together. Christopher was the only man invited, since all of us women trusted him in that way. We felt safe.

I was so grateful that night. My sisters and I were all on a natural high – laughing and walking by the shops, arm-in-arm, as we waited for our table. Christopher was a few steps behind me – and I could feel the energy current shooting through my skin. When seated, he sat across from me, although he never needed to do anything especially obvious for me to be aware of his presence.

It was astronomic.

At that point, I was still burying all of my intense attraction to him, as intoxicating as it all was.

And meanwhile, my friend's feelings for him were growing too.

Then, there was an evanescent moment; and unbeknownst to me, Christopher caught it. What I experienced was a wave of loneliness, which was a new feeling for me. I had never fully felt that emotion; in the past, I would simply fill any emptiness with a man or a distraction of some sort.

But now – sober from the madness – it seemed to hit me like a ton of bricks, and I felt the sadness move through me at the dinner table. My head dropped and I went inward as the sounds in the restaurant receded into the background. I was mistaken to think I was alone in my experience and that everyone else was distracted with their sushi and rumbling conversations. No, Christopher was watching me.

We had carpooled, and as I was saying my goodbyes, he walked up to me.

"I saw you feeling things at dinner. Wanna take a loop around the block?" he said softly.

Surprised, I accepted, and we got in my car and took a late-night drive. As we started talking, he asked me what had happened in the moment he had noticed. I realized I wanted to look at him and be present in our conversation, so I pulled over.

It all flowed as we shared and connected, and out came his truth – he saw me as someone he could do life with. I felt it all too, of course. But my first question to him was about my friend. I asked where he stood with her before giving him **my** full truth – the truth that I saw it **all** with **him**.

Christopher told me they were only friends, so I knew I needed to have a conversation with her to clear it all. We hugged each other. I said goodnight, and told him that I would talk to him again after I cleared it up with my girlfriend.

Everything was happening so quickly – it was like my hands were not even on the wheel, but somehow I was going in the exact direction where I was meant to go. The moment I got to her place, I felt hot. I had never in my life been in this position. I did not know what I was going to say.

As I walked into her bedroom, I received a text from Christopher that said, "I'm with you," and I knew he wanted me to feel supported in taking that big step.

At that moment, I was so sure that he was my person that I went into the conversation with my friend with passion and love and openness. I told her that I had been holding my feelings in, in fear of hurting her, and I wanted her blessing to be with this man who I was pretty sure was my everything person. I knew it was bold, and scary, and I had no idea if I would lose her or both of them.

But it was absolutely beautiful. We both cried because she knew he was not meant for her – and because I too have known rejection, not being chosen – and experienced seeing others happy when I wanted to find my love. She blessed our union fully, and the sweetness oozed around us.

We held each other, and healed a deep sisterhood wound through truth-sharing and receptivity.

When I left her, **I felt like I had wings.**

With the biggest smile on my face and my heart exploding with joy, I called Christopher in the car on the way home and told him I wanted everything with him.

We dove in, headfirst.

My relationship with Chris, thus far, has been the most expansive and transcendent adventure of my life.

We started by FaceTiming and texting all day, sharing stories of our past, expressing fears, and melting into the sweetness of new love – the first honest love I had ever known.

Since Noah all those years ago, I had been putting on a show. I forgot that sex and a relationship were meant to be pleasurable for me, too. I had been numb for so long, unaware of what true love and intimacy meant. I had mastered leaving my body when someone I didn't know was inside of me, fantasizing about being somewhere else.

I thought I needed to contort, deliver, and shut down an entire side of myself in order to satisfy. But I found that I was not merely placed on this earth to give a buzz to men. Rather, I am meant to twirl in delectation, to melt, play and breathe with **all** that I am, and all that life has to offer me.

Through that newness, my first true romantic experience, I began stepping into my sexuality in a way that felt empowering.

I was honest – I told him everything about my past, and that my body was purified of all the old and stagnant. I was open and ready to receive love.

After a couple of weeks of sharing and connecting as much as we could, we were finally ready to spend some time together alone.

I flew to see him in Sebastopol. It was November, and it was the perfect fall atmosphere. When it tips over to winter weather, I usually contract. Over 10 years of New York winters will do that to you. But in Northern California in the autumn, the grounds were wet, the leaves were turning, and the chill was just enough.

Everything felt different. From sitting at the airport gate, to flying, to landing, and then seeing him waiting for me in the parking lot, I felt an awareness and a safety that was newborn.

I had flown to see men many times, but never as my true self – never awake, always in a slumber, desensitized. I had habitually watched my body do things while I was on another planet.

The following is intimate, it is vulnerable and it's real.

My first time with this man was distinctive. I could feel every hair on my body, and could hear the particles in between every breath that I took. Sounds were louder, yet undisturbing, and colors were more scintillating. It felt like the first conscious experience that I had ever had – the first time my eyes were open.

I share our first intimate moments with the intention of bringing you closer, with a whisper and a tiptoe. Trust that you are worthy of fully experiencing a love just like this.

Our first day was peaceful. We took a long ride to the redwood forest. We stayed silent with no music playing, feeling the safekeeping of these precious moments. We talked a great deal too, and then we would find the sweet silent moment return, perfectly placed in between the banter. The pace of our interaction allowed us to integrate and breathe with each other's presence.

The air was brisk, and Chris covered me with his poncho. It was turquoise blue, woven with a multitude of other colors, complementing the brilliant aesthetic of mother nature surrounding us in the forest. We were equally humbled by the holy, wet grounds. We felt the sacredness.

Looking up at the enormity of the redwoods, one might fall into a backbend trying to reach the top with a gaze. Our throats stretched back with our necks, instinctually pausing speech and sound. You could hardly hear a crunch as we walked, and tranquility was rich in the air.

The silence and the magnitude of that bewitching forest was a perfect, awe-inspiring setting for our carefully-paced steps, deep breaths, and roaring hearts.

When Chris held my hand for the first time, a warm current trickled through the lines on my palm that they say represent one's life path. It was a feeling I had not known before. The size of his hands was enormous. He has herculean, yet soft hands. Instantly, I felt shielded. Every finger of his intertwined in mine; it was as if his hands were my hands' match.

We got lost on the way home. It was a weekend; I had turned my phone off, as usual, and there was no service anyway. Neither one of us minded.

I have such a love for small, old, and quirky little towns. Christopher and I just wanted to be near each other and witness all the magic of the place together. We pulled into a little run-down local health food store and asked for directions.

When we got back to where we were staying, the power was out. I loved it, and he did too. We lit some candles and I cooked dinner with two tea lights guiding my hands. The ambiance was intoxicating. I was aching to feel him, and we had not even kissed yet.

In the redwood forest – Christopher let me paint his nails.

It was by far the slowest experience I had ever had with a man, and that was an important lesson. Everything I had known before was like a whirlwind, in flames, with a crash and a burn. It was imperative for me to experience the unhasty deliciousness. It called for presence, trust, and regulation of the nervous system. Our steps were slow, our eye contact was unbreakable, and our breathing was almost visible as it flowed in and out, unhurried.

How often do we experience that kind of slowness in daily life? So much of what we have learned and experienced is about falling, rushing, fire, and quickness. To drop in with someone on the same page as you, discerningly and elegantly, is like the gift of rebirth. You meet yourself in a new way.

While Christopher showered, I walked up to the door and made a peeking gesture. "Can I see?" my eyes asked.

With his hands still in his hair, shampooing his golden locks, he turned and smirked. I had to take a deep breath when I saw between his legs.

I playfully squealed and ran off. He was **perfect.** With the lights still off and nothing but candlelight illuminating our features, Christopher walked out into the room wrapped in a towel. I stood by the staircase, unsure of what to do next.

I suddenly felt my power, and vivaciously said, "I'm going to shower upstairs. Come witness me."

Without breaking my gaze, he nodded, understanding fully.

I brought a candle, and let the steam fill the bathroom. I felt sexier than ever. I had belly chains around my torso, and through the mirror I could see my skin glistening with hot water and the faint illusion of gold, reflecting from the candlelight. I breathed and washed my body.

Chris peered in the doorway, his hands in a pull-up position on the frame, biceps protruding. He kept his eyes on mine and watched for only a few moments before taking a deep breath and walking away.

I waited, curious.

He walked back in 10 seconds later. "I would really like to come in with you," he said surely.

"Come on, then," I replied.

Chris was big in every sense of the word. Solid in every aspect. It was, and still is, overwhelming to be naked with him.

We slowly caressed each other's arms and collarbones, necks and hips. Waists. Backs. Cheeks. Our lips only slightly brushed. We were trying our best to move as slowly as our passion would allow. The steam, the heat, and the lighting kept us in a fantasy-like experience.

I continued, curious, and played with the novelty of it all. We stood in an enormous tub with a seat at the edge, opposite from where the shower head beat down perfectly-heated water on my hair and back.

"Sit? I want you to look at my yoni," I voiced. I'm not sure where that idea came from, but to me it meant something powerful. I had never had someone get to know me down there. I wanted it to happen slowly, with good intention, and with him receiving my permission before any action was taken. I wanted him to be the first.

Chris lowered himself onto the seat and came at eye-level with her. He truly just watched as the water dripped and descended down my inner thigh. We were both moving very steadily, aware of the potency of the moment.

I never could have imagined a connection as succulent.

*Do the things I did in the past make me unworthy to receive **now**?*

It was a question I had asked myself every day for a long time.

I wept after the first time Christopher and I made love. As he held me in a fetal position, he gently kissed my tears. If losing our virginity was based on presence and connection, that was my cherry being popped.

My love with this man opened me up in ways I never thought possible. Through his patience, devotion, and celebration of truth, he helped me heal wounds I once considered permanent. His lovemaking and affection brought me back **into** my body, after all the years I had been absent from it.

We moved to a beautiful island together a short time after committing. We were eager to begin our lives together; eager to manifest our greatest abundance. We both wanted the same things in this life.

Every moment since landing has felt like a dream. Horses roam freely on enormous and vibrant pastures – white horses, black horses, golden brown and sand. The beaches take my breath away every day; the transparent and turquoise shades stun every onlooker. There are waterfalls big and small, with natural pools that you just want to melt into. Trees, abundant with juicy exotic fruits, surround us. We have thriving skin, supported by sunshine and saltwater, and our meals overflow with local ingredients rich in nutrients. We are living our dream.

My first honest relationship is one that, without delay, brought me to my knees. I could write another book about our first year together; but for now, all I will say is that it was not easy. I never understood when people would say, "Partnership takes work," until I experienced this one. We both have wanted to flee at times, and old patterns and triggers have surfaced regularly. We still get up and work, and every day becomes a little bit easier as we get farther away from the old ways.

The love, the fire, and the support and healing in our partnership remains untainted.

As we move through this latest chapter of my life, I want to note that it is not about a fairy tale ending. The journey of truth continues to this day, and I am consistently offered new opportunities from the universe to keep me on my toes.

I am far from perfect, but I am devoted.

There is a new scent on my skin, one that is sensed within moments of a first encounter with me. It keeps wonderful, loving, and **good** people close, rather than pushing them away.

What I have learned above all, is that my love for self is the one true love that I have found along the way. It is the love that I can count on until death, and it is the one that I choose above all, **always**, in **all ways**.

Christopher knows that I will forever choose from my heart, and we honor each other by putting self-care at the top of our priorities. We do not condemn each other for needing space at times, and if one of us should choose to walk away in the future, it would not mean failure or losing our "everything," like we have all heard in love-song lyrics for decades.

We are complete on our own. We love each other profoundly and fully, and yet we bow to each other with deep reverence as we acknowledge the importance of non-attachment.

The love of another is medicine, but the love from oneself is Queen.

Toni Jones, a talented affirmation musician said, "Healing is not my purpose," and a couple of years ago I would not have resonated with that. "Healing is everything to me! My entire life is devoted to healing!" I would scream from the rooftops. I know now that's not true.

We are not here to heal all day, every day. We are here to experience pleasure, to feel love, to give love, to learn, and eat delicious meals and laugh and connect and serve.

During the years of guiding myself back to sanity, I did not fully allow myself to soften into those things. I read nothing but personal growth books, and still I could not fully enjoy or experience the present moment unless I was getting something out of it. Read a novel just to get lost in a beautiful story? Yeah, right.

Today, I choose to just **be**. I choose to enjoy, indulge, create when I feel inspired, and lay my body down to rest when I do not. I choose to not shame myself if I eat a loaf of bread, and I choose to give up the idea that my body needs to be smooth and toned to be perfect. I also choose to take wonderful care of what I was blessed with.

I choose every single day to be loving, and kind, and to tell the truth in every instance. I choose to forgive myself completely for the things I did when I was sad. I choose to accept people for who they are, and I choose to never change my outfit because of what someone might think of it.

I choose to be free, embracing the very essence of the word, in every moment of my life. I choose to allow myself childlike squeals when I see a rainbow or horses on the side of the road.

I choose to love on my body, and I choose to forgive myself when I might fall into old ways of thinking or being. I choose to remind myself that I am absolutely stunning and perfect as is – even when my back rolls are rolling, and my double chin is chinning. **Especially** then.

I also choose to release – every single day – the attachment I once had to my physical appearance. And I choose to dance, sing, and laugh really loud. I also choose to cry hysterically when I need to.

I choose to be soft and acknowledge my purity and I also choose to make delicious love with my partner and bask in my powerful sexual energy. I choose to put on lipstick when I feel in the mood, and I choose to show myself. There are no limits to the choices we get to make, and there is no cap on the abundance of joy available to us. My choices are my tools, and my healing takes care of itself when I luxuriate in my own delight.

AFTERWORD

(A love letter)
by Christopher Callender

It's hard for me to imagine all the entanglements Temima walked herself out of, but here she is, the clearest thinker I know. Bright eyes brimming with loving-kindness. Devoted to growth and her creative purpose.

It's hard for me to imagine how she freed herself, because we share a similar past. In my rebellion against my own inner light, I explored and experimented with the darker aspects of human nature, but for me it's been much harder to free myself. Where I tried to do all my deep work in private, keeping a lifetime of shadows to myself, Temima took a wildly different approach.

When we first met, she had recently committed to radical honesty, learning to be truthful and trustworthy, while I was learning to speak my truth, and to trust. Trust was my deepest wound, my oldest story. I learned early on that people couldn't be trusted. I had seen behind the veil too many times, finding cracks in each luminary's promise. Their facade may have been how they saw themselves, but it wasn't who they were. At best, I found that what people preached was the lesson they were trying to learn. The louder they were about spreading their message, the deeper I looked for their deceptions.

My experience of Temima was different. I didn't know who she was, other than Levi's sister. I didn't know about her following on Instagram or her past. It wasn't until a couple weeks after we first met, when she gave me a ride home from Ojai to LA, that we had a proper conversation. She shocked me by not trying to impress me. She was open about gut-wrenching experiences from her past, she didn't omit facts that could turn people off, and she didn't sensationalize her time with the rich and famous. Instead, she was under-spoken, raw, and even a little nervous as she shared where she was on her journey.

I remember how taken I was by her transparency. Most people I knew obscured or lied about their past. Her radical honesty was refreshing, as well as her humility – the type you only feel in a person who has experienced atonement. I heard the introspection in her voice, the remorse for the pain she caused others, and the love she gave herself, accepting all that she had gone through without any desire to change what happened. She spoke passionately about truth being her most important lesson, but she made it clear that radical honesty was still new for her. She was in no way perfect, but learning every day. She wasn't preaching, she was practicing. For the first time, I found myself believing someone at face value.

It struck me how she had not only been to the bottom, like me, but had explored it in a way I didn't know anyone else understood. It struck me even more how, having been so lost in distortion and dissociation, she was now free of her story's demons.

Reading *Can I Be Honest?*, I see why I'm still stuck in certain areas. Temima's unapologetic excavation of her shadow side shows me how I need to evaluate my own unspoken ways of being. I see where I need to air out my old demons, rather than reject, suppress, avoid or bypass them. If she can liberate herself by coming clean, radically unearthing her past, and owning all the thoughts and feelings the old Sarah Temima would never have said out loud, then any one of us can do the same, each in our own way.

Mima, from you I learned, through experience, that until I name my demons and own my part in creating them, they own me. When I name them, and I see them for what they are – unprocessed emotions and experiences that are set free by the light of awareness – they stop being demons.

Thank you for being a greater lover than I dared to imagine, and for being much more than a lover. Thank you for walking me back into lightness and ease. For showing me it's safe to trust. For believing in me and holding onto us when I tried to kick over the little bucket in our hearts. Thank you for being the leader you are, and the goofball, the sexy mama, the closet nerd, the provocateur, the artist, the joy-monger, the lioness. You're a full-spectrum woman, and I'm proud to stand with you in all your bearings.

As a truth-seeker, you inspire me. As my best friend, the adventures of Poo and Goo crack me up and melt me down. As the mother of my baby girl, your calling to raise women up all around the world starts in our home, and I'm honored to learn what this looks like with you each and every day.

We've done the work, and continue to look at what needs to be seen. We've shed old ways of being, and are learning new ones, free of programming. Now we get to write our stories from an authentic place, on the edge of truth, committed to the present moment.

ILYIY,
Chris

ABOUT THE COVER

Have you ever looked at a piece of art and wondered what it was? Or wondered what was in the artist's mind and how he or she created it? Well I created the art that graces the front cover of *Can I Be Honest?* and it is derived from the sketch on the following page that was generously gifted to me by Artist Natalie Miller.

After re-working and playing around with Natalie's original art piece, and settling on the image that is on the cover, it was interesting to see how different women saw different things. My publisher initially thought it was a ball gown, and at another glance it could reveal a mountain path, or a woman's body. What do you see?

I see a vulnerable woman. I see an assertive woman. I see a woman unafraid to show all of herself, howling at the moon.

My experience with this piece was that it portrayed perfectly the distorted path of woman, sexuality, and our connection to the moon. I always felt so much power from the moon, pulling me and pushing me with its many transformations throughout the month. Sometimes I changed just as many times as she does in a matter of 28 days.

I am beyond grateful for the way Natalie's art guided my creative process for the cover of this book, powerfully showcasing our individuality.

COVER INSPIRATION

© by Natalie Miller

ASCENSION
BY NATALIE MILLER

Ascension is inspired by the changes in life that inevitably come. This piece inspires us to hold deep compassion when we enter a time that asks us to let go. We are allowed to seek guidance, and to remember the essence, the ooze, the slow drip of our souls. May our bodies be a portal to remind us that each new phase births new life for us to experience. May the fear dissipate as we learn to embrace these times. May this piece remind us to come back home to our bodies.

I birthed Ascension following a humbling shadow chapter, only three months after moving to LA. It was my commitment to come back to my body, as an act of forgiveness, after I exited a series of codependent romantic and familial relationships that centered around substance abuse. I have since created a space, the Embodiment Collective, where artists and women can seek refuge.

The Embodiment Collective community mission is to use fine art as an invitation. It invites and encourages muses to move out of performance and artists to move out of perfectionism – and into feeling into our own bodies. By doing that, we are able to create intuitively, based on how we feel and on our own creative aliveness. Through our bodies, we are able to realize that we are so much more than just what the external world sees based on our physical form. We can decide how we want to show up, and who we want to be. We embody the female form as a catalyst for our feelings and sensitivities, as a portal to many other bodies, and as a way to expand.

This piece was gifted to Sarah as an acknowledgment of her embodiment of the divine feminine in her own life – raw, honest, alive. It is a gift given to a sister of the Embodiment Collective.

Natalie Miller

Follow the practice:
theembodimentcollective.life
@the.embodimentcollective

ABOUT THE AUTHOR

Sarah Temima is a fashion designer, entrepreneur, creative director, writer, and singer-songwriter. She does most of her work from the comfort of her tiny island home as a dedicated introvert. Sarah founded Love On Collections in 2018 in Los Angeles, California – a clothing brand now adored by thousands across the globe.

Love On's designs focus on a "hold" that women can't seem to live without. Testimonials roll in daily with praise for the intricately designed pieces. Her everyday hobbies include walking in nature, cooking, swimming, reading, singing, and writing. She currently lives in Hawaii with her partner. They are expecting their first child.

Sign up to be notified about new releases at Loveoncollections.com

Follow Sarah's journey on her personal Instagram account @sarahtemima, and stay in the loop with new designs and collections in the works through Love On's official Instagram, @loveoncollections.

Visit sarahtemima.com to join those on a similar path, sign up for Sarah's newsletter, and to purchase signed copies of *Can I Be Honest?* along with a very special journal.